700028557542

D1420751

RACING POST
100 Greatest Races

RACING POST
100 Greatest Races

edited by
Nicholas Godfrey
with Steve Dennis

highdown

Photographs: Gerry and Mark Cranham, Edward Whitaker, Martin Lynch, Caroline Norris, George Selwyn, Alec Russell, Bill Selwyn, John Crofts, Bernard Parkin, John Beasley, Ian Stewart, S Kikkawa, Empics, Getty Images, Allsport, Benoit Photo, Central Press Photos, Action Images, Sportsphoto, Universal Pictorial Press, Illustrated London News, Press Association, APRH, Daily Mirror, Racing Post.

Please note that every effort has been made to find and to credit the copyright holders of the photographs and we apologise for any omissions.

For their invaluable assistance, special thanks are given to: Tracey Scarlett, Robin Gibson, John Randall, Martin Smethurst, Jo Yarborough, Susannah Messer-Bennetts, Amy Bennett, Victor Jones and Sean Magee

WORCESTERSHIRE COUNTY COUNCIL	
754	
Bertrams	28.01.06
798.4	£18.99
RE	

Published in 2005 by Highdown,
an imprint of Raceform Ltd.,
Compton, Newbury, Berkshire, RG20 6NL
Raceform Ltd is a wholly owned subsidiary of Trinity-Mirror plc

Copyright © Raceform 2005

All rights reserved. No part of this publication may be reproduced, stored in a retrieval system, or transmitted in any form or by any means, electronic, mechanical, photocopying, recording, or otherwise, without the prior written permission of the publishers.

A CIP catalogue record for this book is available from the British Library.

ISBN 1-905156-14-6

Designed by Robin Gibson and Tracey Scarlett
Picture research by Victor Jones and Tracey Scarlett
Printed in Great Britain by William Clowes Ltd, Beccles, Suffolk

RACING POST

100 Greatest Races

contents

about the contributors

100 Greatest Races features work from the *Racing Post*'s top writers, both journalists employed on the staff at the paper and occasional columnists alike.

The book's editor Nicholas Godfrey is the paper's associate editor (features) and Sunday columnist, having previously fulfilled many other roles in 18 years at the paper, including reporter, news editor, features editor and deputy editor. In 2005 he wrote the series On The Racing Road, featuring reports from around the globe.

Assistant editor Steve Dennis, the paper's deputy features editor, is also responsible for the popular series A Life After Racing.

However, this book is a real team effort. Other contributors are renowned as the foremost in their field, among them John Randall, racing's number-one historian, and Tony Morris, the sport's leading bloodstock writer.

Essays on the top ten have also been contributed by a handful of *Racing Post* regulars who are among the best-known names in the business, among them a number of former racing journalists of the year in David Ashforth, George Ennor, Rodney Masters and Brough Scott. Also featured in this section are two of the *Post*'s brightest talents in Peter Thomas and James Willoughby, while another, Lee Mottershead, joins Howard Wright, one of the most respected industry commentators, among those who have written about races slightly lower down.

Dennis, Ennor, Godfrey, Mottershead and Randall are between them responsible for the pen-portraits of the races between numbers 21 and 100.

The *Post*'s revered team of foreign correspondents – Tony O'Hehir (Ireland), Desmond Stoneham (France), Dan Farley (USA) and Syd Brennan (Australia) – have also submitted their own top tens of races from their respective nations.

Many members of the *Post* team feature elsewhere, including leading columnists Paul Haigh and Sir Clement Freud, chief race analyst Graham Dench, bloodstock aficionado Rachel Pagones, letters editor Martin Smethurst and Irish-based correspondent Michael Clower.

Other contributors include three names to have graced the training ranks with distinction over the years in Ian Balding, Bill O'Gorman and Mark Johnston.

Many of the interviews included in the book's various sections were conducted by *Post* staffers Amy Bennett and Susannah Messer-Bennetts.

Finally, like its predecessor *100 Favourite Racehorses*, this book is illustrated by the work of a plethora of excellent photographers. The majority of photographs, however, are taken from the libraries of Edward Whitaker, the *Post*'s much-decorated staff man, and the esteemed Gerry Cranham.

foreword
Lester Piggott

NO two people can ever agree about exactly what makes a horse race so memorable that it deserves the label 'great'.

It's not simply a matter of a desperately close finish, or a long-drawn-out battle: the 100 races recalled in this book include 'Eclipse first, the rest nowhere' as well as dead-heats and wafer-thin short-head verdicts.

Nor is it necessarily a question of quality. Some races – the 1913 Derby, or 1956 and 1967 Grand Nationals, for example – have found a place on account of some bizarre incident, while others have had greatness thrust upon them through their wider significance, where the bare result is of less consequence than the occasion.

The 1990 Breeders' Cup Mile that I won on Royal Academy, voted no.9 in the final poll among *Racing Post* readers, comes into that category. Throughout my riding career I never tended to get particularly elated after any big-race victory – my attitude was always that 'a race is a race' and move on to the next one – but that day at Belmont Park was undeniably special. I had returned to race-riding only 12 days earlier, and to win the richest prize of my career on a horse trained by Vincent O'Brien, with whom I had shared so many wonderful moments and who had been very instrumental in my comeback, was exceptionally satisfying.

My win in the 1984 St Leger on Commanche Run (no.100) was another example of the occasion being more significant than the individual race, as that win brought me my record 28th Classic.

By contrast, each of my three Derby winners in the book is here on account of the race itself. Sir Ivor in 1968 (no.72) showed a turn of foot that astonished even me, while the other two

live in the memory because of their desperate finishes. Roberto short-heading Rheingold in 1972 was voted as high as 14, but for me The Minstrel beating Hot Grove a neck in 1977 (no.32) was much more satisfying. Roberto had needed all that encouragement in the final furlong as he simply wasn't putting in enough effort, while The Minstrel on Derby Day was as brave as any horse I ever rode.

I suppose the 1990 Breeders' Cup would have to be my own greatest moment, but objectively a race can only be considered truly great if it produces an exceptional performance from an individual horse, and there is no doubt that the two finest performances I ever saw were from Sea-Bird in the 1965 Prix de l'Arc de Triomphe (no.16), and Arazi in the 1991 Breeders' Cup Juvenile (no.15).

At Longchamp, Sea-Bird took on perhaps the finest international field that had ever been assembled and ran right away from them in the straight, winning by six lengths despite veering to the left in the final furlong. It was a sensational performance, and so was that of Arazi at Churchill Downs. Slow out of the gate, he seemed in trouble going down the back stretch, then produced a startling change of gear to cut his way through the field and go further and further clear in the home straight, running out an astounding winner.

100 Greatest Races will revive so many memories of the big moments and famous occasions, but for me those two races remain outstanding. I rode in both, so could feel at first hand the magnitude of the performances. In both cases, what the horses did on the day was unbelievable. It's as simple as that!

introduction
Nicholas Godfrey

JUST how, exactly, do we follow that? That was the question some of us at the *Racing Post* were asking as we looked back at the success of the two reader polls we had run in the early months of 2003 and 2004.

First had come 100 Racing Greats, in which readers voted the legendary Vincent O'Brien as horseracing's greatest figure of all time. Then, 12 months later in a ballot that resulted in another victory for Ireland, Arkle was identified as the most popular horse in racing history in 100 Favourite Racehorses.

If reader response is anything to go by, both series were massively popular and both attracted thousands of votes, an unusually high proportion of them accompanied by letters explaining the many and varied choices. As we looked ahead to 2005, the question was never *if* we were going to run another similar poll; the question was only what it would be.

The answer? Having identified the greatest individual and the most popular horse, we would go for the hat-trick by asking readers to pinpoint the greatest race of all time involving horses trained in Britain and Ireland.

There are those who dislike such retrospective exercises, questioning their efficacy with particular reference to horseracing, a sport in which a huge amount of the interest is focused on attempting to forecast what will happen in the future.

Yet while they are entirely welcome to their opinion, such a rigidly utilitarian approach seems to deny the richest of histories – and plenty of *Racing Post* readers seemed to enjoy another chance to remember glorious days gone by.

That's how, starting in December 2004 and for two months afterwards, my colleague Steve Dennis, who has acted as assistant editor on this book, found himself totting up votes received in the post and via email as readers offered their nominations.

Undoubtedly the result might have been slightly different if the exercise had been repeated even a few months later, but this is how it happened then: the 100 greatest races in the history of horseracing as voted by *Racing Post* readers between December 2004 and February 2005.

Well, actually, it wasn't quite as simple as that. Whereas 100 Favourite Racehorses was designed deliberately as purely a popularity contest – it just happened that the greatest was also the most popular – the title of 100 Greatest Races implied some objective qualitative assessment.

Therefore, alongside the readers' votes, in a bid to ensure some degree of historical perspective, a specially convened *Racing Post* panel also played a part in the process. Racing's greatest historian John Randall, the world's foremost bloodstock expert Tony Morris and *Racing Post* editor Chris Smith joined Steve and me in submitting our own ideas alongside those of the readers, though these were given much less significance in the final list of 100.

Thousands answered our initial request for their nominations; more again participated when telephone lines and text messaging were introduced to sort out the top ten, the final order of which was determined entirely by readers' votes, the *Post* panel having no further involvement at that stage.

Once again, although the concept was straightforward, there were rules. Every reader was allowed just one vote each, naming their 1-2-3 in order, after which we tallied up the scores, with first choices earning more than second, a second choice more than a third.

Every race selected had to involve at least one horse trained in either Britain or Ireland, something that gained enormous significance when Arazi's breathtaking Breeders' Cup Juvenile success at Churchill Downs in 1991 started to gain support. The race *was* eligible – but only because of the presence in the field of a long-forgotten Richard Hannon-trained colt named Showbrook, who finished 14th of 14, a country mile behind the unforgettable winner. (He was even six lengths behind the horse who came 13th!)

Readers were also invited to write letters in support of their first choice – and those who did, as in the previous poll, gained a small points bonus for their selection.

The *Racing Post* letters team of Martin Smethurst and Jo Yarborough sifted them, eventually picking what they considered the best five out of the hundreds to receive a small prize. Those five are reproduced in this volume, as are the selections of a host of racing celebrities.

While identifying a favourite racehorse was necessarily a subjective choice reflecting a personal preference, being asked to pinpoint the greatest example of something is a less straightforward concept.

What, exactly, constitutes a great race? Everyone who bothered to vote presumably has their own idea of what it is, and doubtless we all applied our own criteria when making our judgements.

Whatever basis readers used for selecting their top three, enough of them participated to produce the list of 100 included here. Indeed, a total of 273 races received at least one third-placed vote, with an understandable bias towards races held in the last three decades, within the lifespan of the majority of *Racing Post* readers.

The top ten was a wondrous list, featuring some of the greatest names in racing history and some of the most memorable clashes, among them Crisp and Red Rum, Grundy v Bustino, Dancing Brave, Dawn Run and Royal Academy. How could anyone be expected to choose between them?

In order to help readers make up their minds, a team of the *Post*'s best writers penned essays about these exalted contests. These included pieces by a number of the best-known names in racing journalism, such as former sportswriter of the year Brough Scott, former racing journalists of the year David Ashforth, George Ennor and Rodney Masters, and the newer stars of the field, Peter Thomas and James Willoughby.

Alongside these, we have also added extended pieces about the bottom half of the top 20, a list that comprises some unforgettable contests in its own right, such as Red Rum's third National, the Guineas clash between Brigadier Gerard and Mill Reef, and Roberto's Derby, notable primarily for the superhuman efforts of the winning rider Lester Piggott.

Among writers whose work is included here are the aforementioned pair of John Randall and Steve Dennis, without either of whom it is doubtful this project would ever have been completed.

Besides these extended essays on numbers 11-20, this book also features a number of new items, including top tens from abroad by the *Racing Post*'s hugely respected team of foreign correspondents, and personal choices from other staff writers and occasional contributors to the paper.

This is how North American-based greats such as Secretariat, Affirmed and Dr. Fager appear in these pages alongside Australian superstars Kingston Town, Phar Lap and Carbine. It is also how the 1977 Champion Hurdle, somehow ignored by both readers and panel (I know, I'm as culpable as anybody), gets a look-in, thanks to my esteemed colleague Graham Dench.

I hope I have managed to do justice to the greatest clash involving two of the horses in that race, Night Nurse and Monksfield, when they dead-heated in the 1977 Templegate Hurdle, a race that, almost unbelievably, was practically forgotten within the hour as it was followed immediately by Red Rum's third National.

However, admirable though that race was, I did not vote for it as my own personal number one. Instead, I selected the Breeders' Cup Turf of 2003 at Santa Anita, a race most of us probably remember as a thrilling battle between High Chaparral and Falbrav, even though another horse, the US-trained Johar, shared the spoils with the former.

While I have suggested that attempting to isolate the greatest race of all time suggests a degree of objectivity, I have to admit this involved a large dose of subjectivity.

I was lucky enough to be present under the Santa Anita sun that day, and will never forget the excitement of the last couple of furlongs as those two bullish battlers gave everything they had, nor the sense of incredulity when it emerged that a third horse, a vile interloper that had somehow gone unnoticed, had so nearly mugged them both. Racing thrills don't get any better.

But that's just my opinion, and I didn't have the final say. According to *Racing Post* readers, there were 11 greater races in history, and, frankly, I could not have quibbled if any one of them had come out on top.

The final ballot involving the top ten lasted two weeks. It was pretty close between the top six for a few days, before the top four pulled away.

Dancing Brave's finishing burst took the 1986 Arc into fourth, while the race known forever simply by the names of its two main protagonists, Grundy and Bustino, took third, making it, unsurprisingly, the greatest Flat race in history.

It was only well into the second week of voting that it become clear that a jump race would be voted number one; only in the final days was your ultimate choice established. Red Rum may have overhauled Crisp in the 1973 Grand National, but the 1989 Cheltenham Gold Cup fought all the way to the line. What else would you expect of a race involving Desert Orchid?

RACING POST

100 Greatest Races

Notes on the text: All writers are credited in full on numbers 1-20; where initials are used on 21-100, the writers are Steve Dennis (SD), George Ennor (GE), Nicholas Godfrey (NG), Lee Mottershead (LM) and John Randall (JR). All photographic credits appear with the picture

Gerry and Mark Cranham

1

Desert Orchid's Gold Cup

CHELTENHAM, MARCH 16, 1989

1. Desert Orchid 5-2f
2. Yahoo 25-1
3. Charter Party 14-1

Winning Owner: Richard Burridge
Trainer: David Elsworth
Jockey: Simon Sherwood
Distance: 1½l, 8l
Also ran: Bonanza Boy (4th), West Tip (last), Ballyhane (bd), Cavvies Clown (ref), Pegwell Bay (pu), Slalom (f), Ten Plus (f, dead), The Thinker (f), Carvill's Hill (f), Golden Freeze (f). 13 ran.

Desert Orchid and Yahoo set off up the unforgiving Cheltenham hill after the last

The 1989
Cheltenham
Gold Cup

by Peter
Thomas

In some arenas, inclement weather might be

viewed as putting a damper on proceedings. At the World Sunbathing Championships, for example, or among the softies at Royal Ascot, any conditions but clear skies and sunshine are often regarded as detracting from the spectacle and making a mockery of the form.

Among followers of jump racing, however, no true act of heroism can be acclaimed without the presence of one or more of heavy rain, torrential rain, hail or snow. When Cheltenham Gold Cup day 1989 delivered all of the above by the bucketload, we should have known that greatness was about to emerge from the gloom and wipe its wellingtons on the doormat of Turf history.

Fortunately, the same isobars that set the scene for the triumph and the tragedy of the day were not enough to frighten off its principal players. Desert Orchid – an Olivier among equines – was the undisputed star, but even if it may not have been the best field ever assembled for the showpiece, let nobody claim anything other than that the supporting cast twinkled with quality.

In a field of 13, there were two previous Gold Cup heroes in the shape of The Thinker and Charter Party, the 1988 runner-up Cavvies Clown, the classy and progressive Ten Plus, Welsh National and Racing Post Chase winner Bonanza Boy, and the hugely talented, if alarmingly flawed, Carvill's Hill. Oh, and a 25-1 hunter-chase type by the name of Yahoo.

Brown trilbies, hurled skyward in jubilation, fell like righteous rain on the Cheltenham lawn

To get the better of 12 of them and some of the vilest conditions ever to grace a Festival would take an act of some courage. In the event, it took more courage than many of us had ever seen in one place at one time.

The weather had already played a part in setting the scene long before dawn broke on the Thursday of the Festival. As the elements steadily worked their way into the ground, speculation grew that Desert Orchid might duck the Gold Cup. It wasn't just that he wouldn't be best suited by the mud. Or that he had always performed below par when asked to tackle the rigours of Cheltenham. Or that the three miles and two furlongs would stretch his stamina to the limit. It was all of the above.

However, his trainer David Elsworth jutted his jaw and stuck to the plan. A week before the Festival, the galloping grey was put on rails leading straight to the toughest test of his career. The racing world doffed its cap to the sporting Elsworth for turning a good race into a potentially great one.

Although he denies it now, surely even 'Elzee' must have wavered a little on the morning of the race when he saw snow settling on the course and imagined the "Dessie brought down by loose penguin" headline in the following day's *Racing Post*.

As temperatures rose just above bitter, snow was followed by hours of driving rain and sleet. Among a vast crowd looking for an act of heroic achievement, none would have been surprised to see Hannibal breasting Cleeve Hill with his elephants.

Janice Coyle keeps a tight hold on Desert Orchid as he stands in the winner's enclosure at Cheltenham

Billy Stickland / Allsport

But the maverick trainer stood his ground with a pronouncement that every trainer of an exceptional performer would do well to jot down and inwardly digest: "The ground is horrible and conditions are all against him, but he is the best horse."

Between the last two fences, that pronouncement looked set to come back and haunt Elsworth. It seemed for all the world as though the story of the race would be the unlikely, grinding success of Yahoo, a chaser not fit to oil Desert Orchid's hooves in the normal course of events, but a jumper and a stayer of the old school. It would have been remembered, but not as great.

It's hard to imagine now, but the ground at Cheltenham was genuinely heavy, in the same way that mud is genuinely brown. Only after a midday inspection was the course ruled to be fit. If this was to be a great race, it would not be a pretty one.

All morning, I'd watched the weather do its worst, and shared the common doubts about the trip and the ground and the track, but when 'Dessie' drifted to 3-1 shortly before the off, I felt so insulted on his behalf that I had to step in with a bet that I figured might make this a special Gold Cup for me. I needn't have bothered; I think every one of the 50,000-plus people in Prestbury Park that day, bet or no bet, ended by hauling the sport's best-loved performer up the final hill, turning the race into something special by the sheer force of collective will.

Desert Orchid set out to take the fight to the opposition. If he was going to be beaten, he seemed to be saying, he would be taking a few down with him.

Simon Sherwood had him jumping sweetly in front from the start, saving energy by fluency, but he was joined by Ten Plus and Cavvies Clown heading out on to the final circuit and passed by the former at the 14th of the 22 fences. Fulke Walwyn's class act was still motoring, but sadly he was to provide the tragic strand to this epic tale, crashing out, with mortal injuries, three from home. Sherwood claimed to have had Ten Plus comfortably in his sights anyway, but the ensuing lung-bursting battle with Yahoo was to have no comfort zone for either.

Tom Morgan sent Yahoo up the inner nearing the second-last, forging ahead and seeming to have pulled his rival's teeth, but Desert Orchid rallied with a force that moved Sherwood to say afterwards: "I've never known a horse so brave. He hated every step of the way in the ground and dug as deep as he could possibly go."

At the last, he was almost level with Yahoo. Gathered up and straightened by Sherwood after the fence, he gasped one final time for air and summoned up a withering surge – in reality not much faster than a plod – that took him one and a half mud-splattered lengths clear.

Brown trilbies, hurled skyward in jubilation, fell like righteous rain on the Cheltenham lawn as one exceptional horse crossed the line ahead of a very brave one whose role had been as the yeast of competition, to ferment excellence. Charter Party, for the record, was eight lengths back in third.

The faithful and the converted welcomed Desert Orchid back to the sodden winner's enclosure in a manner that was supposed to be the preserve of the Irish, but the reception wasn't simply for a hero, it was for a race that took the notion of greatness, captured its essence in one stirring image and inked it like a tattoo on the arm of horseracing.

Desert Orchid what they said

DAVID ELSWORTH
Desert Orchid's trainer

"If the Gold Cup were run at Kempton, Dessie would have won it four times but, as it's run at Cheltenham, I never thought the old boy would do it.

"On the day he won it, poor old Richard Burridge was taking the responsibility of ownership pretty heavily and, like all of us, he had the horse's welfare paramount in his thoughts.

"He wasn't sure the horse would be able to go through the ground, but I knew he could cope with it and he was also the best jumper in the field. So when the media started asking me whether or not we would run, I told them of course we would.

"What nearly did for Dessie was the final bend, as he never seemed to get the wind in his sails coming round it. But I thought he would win when he got to Yahoo at the final fence – he always fought up the hill and he was in one of his most cussed moods that day. The celebrations afterwards were marvellous. It was a wonderful day and a great race."

JANICE COYLE
Desert Orchid's groom

"That day was full of drama from beginning to end because after the ground went heavy there was a doubt whether he'd run – though throughout David Elsworth was adamant he would.

"I watched, Henrietta Knight-style, from between the fingers of my right hand clasped over my face. I was down by the final fence. Yahoo was in the lead. Our horse was closing. The last I saw they were locked together. Then the commentator screamed 'Dessie's done it. Dessie's done it'.

"Everything went crazy. I felt so proud. As you'd expect the race took quite a lot out of him, and it was a couple of days before he was fully back to his best.

"It also took that time to clean the last of the mud off his coat. You don't know how much I've been aching for our Gold Cup to win this vote."

SIMON SHERWOOD
Desert Orchid's jockey

"I thought he was two stone below his best left-handed, and, sure enough, at most fences he popped out to the right.

"Yahoo cruised by on the final bend

and I thought the game was up, but once we were in a straight line Dessie knew what had to be done.

"Many believed the ground was against him, and yes, he didn't like it, but in the end I believe it worked in his favour because he'd the guts to cope with it better than the rest. He was utterly bloody-minded in his will to win.

"As we came upsides Yahoo, Desert Orchid veered left to confront him. If I'd not made a move to straighten him up, he'd have barged poor Yahoo off to the silver ring.

"That was an indication of his competitive spirit: that's what made him a champion. Once he'd edged ahead there was no possible way he was going to be beaten. He was that stubborn."

"Although Yahoo went on turning for home, I never lost confidence we'd win. Desert Orchid didn't like left-handed bends. He was like a yacht needing to rearrange its sail.

"Once in a straight line I knew he'd pick up. Replay his previous races at Cheltenham and you'll see after that final bend he'd stay on.

"I'm thrilled the public voted for his Gold Cup. I remember feeling so proud to be part of such a great race. I still do."

TOM MORGAN
Yahoo's jockey

"Desert Orchid was such a streetfighter, he was the last horse I'd pick to slog out a finish against.

"Up the run-in Desert Orchid came level with us, then drifted left to eyeball Yahoo. That was his style. Yahoo was brave and battled hard, bless him, but I knew we'd a problem pitched against such a great horse.

"The noise from the crowd was deafening. I'd ridden in most big races, but I'd not heard anything like that. When we jumped the last it was almost as if the volume was turned up from a power of zero to ten in half a stride. I wonder still how many were cheering for Yahoo!

"Desert Orchid responded to the crowd like no other horse I've known. Their cheers drove him forward. As we pulled up, I reached over and gave him a pat. It was some performance on a track he didn't like, on ground he hated. I remember thinking at the time that, although we'd been beaten, it was a privilege to be involved in such a terrific race."

Desert Orchid in front early on, with (from left) Ten Plus, Yahoo, West Tip, Charter Party, and The Thinker

David Cannon / Allsport

Daily Mirror

**Desert Orchid is
on everyone's
Christmas card list**

Could it all have been so different?

WAS Desert Orchid a fortunate winner of the greatest race? Most participants in the 1989 Gold Cup suggest the outcome could possibly have been different had leader Ten Plus, who was fancied to give Fulke Walwyn a fifth win in the race, not misjudged the third-last fence and taken a fall that was to end his life. His near-hind leg was fractured.

A grand, old-fashioned chaser, typical of the many stars trained by Walwyn, Ten Plus was ridden by Kevin Mooney, now assistant trainer to Barry Hills. Stamina was the forte of the third favourite, who had set up a sequence of four straight wins in his build-up to the Festival, often by forcing the pace.

"We'd taken the lead off Desert Orchid with a circuit to go," Mooney recalls. "My horse was such a thorough stayer I wanted to make it a true test of stamina. In the hours up to the race they'd been pumping water off the course. The ground was horrible.

"As I went by Desert Orchid he was clearly hating the ground. I thought there was no way he could win. Ten Plus was a couple of lengths ahead when we came down. I'd got a breather into him after the previous ditch, he was travelling nicely. But all credit to Desert Orchid. He was so brave to come back and win when everything looked against him.

"We don't know if Ten Plus would have won had he stood up, but I certainly wouldn't want to take anything away from Desert Orchid. He had everything you'd look for in a chaser."

David Elsworth readily concedes the misfortune to Ten Plus did spoil the day for him. "It was a horrible thing to happen and took the shine off the race," he says. "I felt for his connections."

Desert Orchid what they said

NICKY HENDERSON
Trainer

"I think it has been fascinating reading about some of these epic battles. Bustino and Grundy was probably the best Flat race, but Desert Orchid's Gold Cup win was a great race. I watched it from where I watch every race at Cheltenham, on the lawn in front of the grandstand, and the atmosphere was great. He was a very, very popular horse, so he was the horse that everybody wanted to win. Rather like Arkle before him, these horses are around for a while so they become really the public's horse."

DAVID NICHOLSON
Trainer of third-placed Charter Party

"My recollections are that the ground was very wet and I sat next to David Elsworth at lunch and he was thinking of withdrawing him. I said to him: 'Don't be silly, you're here now'. I watched from the lawn as I always did and when he passed the post it was huge – it was just like Dawn Run again."

LORCAN WYER
Rider of more than 600 winners, including Festival victors Omerta and Barton

"I watched the race with mixed emotions as I was cheering on Tom Morgan, who was riding Yahoo in the race. I was giving him a good shout from the weighroom as I was a great admirer of his talent over the years, but all I could hear was everyone shouting 'Go on Dessie, go on Dessie', and I remember turning around and shouting back, 'Which one is Dessie?!'

"Every individual contest at Cheltenham is packed with a whole range of emotions but that race was particularly special. He was a super ambassador for the game and what he may have lacked in sheer class, he made up for with his super jumping ability and tremendous guts and determination."

DESSIE SCAHILL
Ireland's best-known racecourse commentator

"I remember him coming to the last and the ground was so testing one felt he wasn't going to get home, but his class, coupled with the unbelievable roar of the crowd, got him home to beat outsider Yahoo. He was such a King George specialist and the people's champion at the time, but to become one of the greats he had to win a Gold Cup, although it was far from a vintage race that year. Not too many people cared, as it was the popular result."

RICHARD DUNWOODY
Rider of third-placed Charter Party

"It was a very, very wet day and everyone was wondering whether Desert Orchid would run or not and there was a huge amount of hype. I was really happy with Charter Party finishing third as a lot of people had written him off, but at the same time it was great to be part of the race and witness the scenes afterwards, and I was chuffed to bits for 'Sharky' [Simon Sherwood]. There were unbelievable scenes, but then I remember Kevin Mooney came in, in floods of tears after his mount Ten Plus had been killed. Nothing summed up the highs and lows more of National Hunt."

JENNY PITMAN
Gold Cup-winning trainer of Golden Freeze

"There are so many great champions, but some live longest in the memory, and he was definitely one of them. Maybe it was because he was grey, but he had so much courage and tried so hard for you.

"I was standing on the lawn in front of the stand, I was struggling to see but the crowd was letting me know what was happening, they were going mad. The Irish always try to make the most noise, but I made up for about ten of them, cheering him on. When he came in, he got the sort of reception a pop star does. He was National Hunt's chart-topper and heart-stopper."

PETER SCUDAMORE
Rider of fourth-placed Bonanza Boy

"Simon Sherwood was staying with me, and it started snowing on the morning of the race, which I was delighted about as I thought it gave Bonanza Boy an outstanding chance, whereas Simon wasn't. It was a very emotional moment and it was fantastic to see a great champion be crowned where he deserved to be – you can win however many King Georges, but the Gold Cup is where you'll be judged. I was just really happy for Simon, who's a great friend."

How the *Racing Post* reported on the 1989 Cheltenham Gold Cup

Racing Post Friday 17 March 1989

THE DREAM COMES TRUE

PAUL HAYWARD

HE did it. Desert Orchid did it. Amid tumultuous scenes at Cheltenham yesterday the nation's favourite horse landed the £100,000 Tote Gold Cup with a final flourish that will live on in legend.

But once again pure glory and pain were potently mixed. The race, which will have set the statue-makers to work on one of the great steeplechasers, also claimed the life of Fulke Walwyn's Ten Plus, who broke a leg and had to be put down.

The euphoria that greeted Desert Orchid was reminiscent of Dawn Run's reception here three years ago. David Elsworth pushed his way through the crowds to the winner's enclosure in a flood of tears and spent at least a minute and a half trying to persuade the policeman on the gate that he was the winning trainer.

The race reached its climax where it should – at the very end. Simon Sherwood, who rode a craftsman's race, had given his mount a break on the second circuit but came with a driving, gripping run again on ground that was testing the very spirit.

"He absolutely hated this going but still acted on it," said Sherwood. "He's two stones better on good ground. Yahoo jumped the last in front, but I'd given him a breather and knew I could get back at him. Dessie just kept digging and digging.

"Yahoo was still going well but I heard the roar of the crowd and just put my head down. I put my head down and kept kicking."

At the line the distance between the winner and Yahoo was just a length and a half, with last year's winner Charter Party eight lengths back in third.

Desert Orchid had never won in five attempts at Cheltenham and owner Richard Burridge was in pessimistic mood when he arrived at the track after heavy snow and sleet had fallen in the morning.

Burridge, however, played down rumours that he had implored his trainer to withdraw the horse.

"Absolutely not," he said. "When I got here I was worried because the ground was appalling, but I spoke to David and he said we would win. This horse produces a great emotional response in the public and it's a privilege to be part of it. He's brilliant."

Elsworth was surrounded by a swarm of bodies in the winner's enclosure and found words, so redundant after such a spectacle, hard to come by. "The ground didn't worry me," he said. "Next year, anything could have happened. I told Richard it would be all right."

The Gold Cup has a history whole nations would be envious of, but this running was as eventful as any. Ireland's young pretender Carvill's Hill, Slalom, The Thinker and, of course, Ten Plus all fell. Coral estimated that the result cost them nearly £500,000 but Ladbrokes' Mike Dillon called it only "a small loser".

The losers and the fallen were left in the mud, but this was the day all of racing wanted. It may be decades before we see such a thing again.

Racing Post Friday 17 March 1989

INDOMITABLE SPIRIT GIVES DESSIE CUP OF JOY

GEORGE ENNOR

DESERT ORCHID'S performance in winning the Cheltenham Gold Cup yesterday was one of the most magnificent displays it has been my privilege to see.

The marvellous grey hated the dreadful, rain-soaked conditions from start to finish, according to Simon Sherwood, but such is his unquenchable enthusiasm and determination that yet again he fought back to a great and glorious victory after all had seemed lost and Yahoo had looked certain to beat him.

But this superb display was hit by tragedy as Ten Plus was killed when he fell three from home. Horses sometimes pay a dreadfully heavy price.

And who is to say what might have happened if Ten Plus had not fallen and broken a leg when in the lead at that third-last fence? He had taken up the running at the water jump second time round, and already the field were well and truly on the stretch behind him.

We had lost Golden Freeze at the sixth, Carvill's Hill (Ken Morgan dislocated a collarbone) at the next and The Thinker at the tenth. Bonanza Boy was struggling to hold his place and gradually others started to drop off the pace.

Pegwell Bay was struggling at the top of the hill; West Tip was feeling his years; and Cavvies Clown, who had gone up and down the field like a yo-yo, was on the retreat.

Six fences from home we were down to six serious contenders. Ten Plus was a couple of lengths in front of Desert Orchid, with Yahoo next alongside Charter Party. Then came the improving Ballyhane with Slalom close up.

Slalom fell at that sixth fence from home and going to the third-last Ten Plus was holding his lead and going strongly.

Then the cruellest of cuts. Ten Plus fell and broke a hind fetlock, bringing down Ballyhane, who was fifth, and Desert Orchid was left in front again.

He had made almost all the running, disputing it at the first with Bonanza Boy before going clear at the second, until Ten Plus went past him, and now he was back in command with only Yahoo close enough to look a serious threat.

Charter Party had given his all three out, and as they ran round the home turn to the second-last Yahoo seemed to have taken Desert Orchid's measure.

He jumped that fence half a length in front and started to stretch that advantage as they ran to the final fence, taking an advantage of perhaps a length and a half.

He really did look uncatchable, but we had reckoned without Desert Orchid. No, perhaps we had not reckoned without him, but even so it really looked as if the tenacity of the spirit might be beaten by the reality of the flesh.

Yahoo had only to keep going as he had been and the names of John Edwards, Tom Morgan and owner Alan Parker looked set to take their places on the roll of honour.

But as the 22nd and final fence drew remorselessly nearer, the shading on the picture began to alter. If there had been any light it would have started to shift away a bit from Yahoo and gone back to take Desert Orchid into focus as well.

For Yahoo, having run by far the race of his life, was beginning to feel the strain and Desert Orchid's determination was forcing him back.

At the final fence Yahoo was no more than half a length in front and he was evidently exhausted. Desert Orchid was not exactly running away either, but he was closing on Yahoo with every stride.

For a moment, as they started up that final, slogging hill, Yahoo looked as if he might hold on, and even when Desert Orchid drew alongside he did all he could to keep even a nostril in front.

But he just could not do it. Sherwood had, as he said later, to dig deeper than he had ever done in any of his previous eight unbeaten rides on Desert Orchid, and his marvellous partner answered every call.

Yahoo finally had to cry enough 50 yards from the line and when they reached that final marker the grey was a length and a half in front, Charter Party, delighting his trainer David Nicholson – "I always said I'd have him back and maybe they won't knock last year's race now" – was eight lengths back in third, with Bonanza Boy and West Tip distances back in fourth and fifth. They were the only others to finish.

David Elsworth's first one-word response afterwards was a simple "fantastic". It truly was. The trainer added: "Three times I thought he was beaten but he fought back like the true professional he is. This is a very special moment. He'll now run at Liverpool in the Chivas Regal Cup, and go for the Whitbread again."

You cannot leave the race without a thought of sympathy for Yahoo and his team. "I thought he would win halfway between the last two," said John Edwards, "but then he just started to tie up as they got to the last."

However much we can rightly sympathise with the Yahoo camp, and it would be totally wrong not to, and however much our hearts go out to Fulke Walwyn, Basil Thwaites and Kevin Mooney over Ten Plus, it was inevitably Desert Orchid's day.

Red Rum and Crisp's battle in 1973 was the

greatest and most agonising Grand National of them all. It was the moment when Red Rum began his career as the ultimate Aintree hero, but on the day the first emotion was to mourn the impossibly heroic Crisp in defeat.

Crisp was conceding 23lb, more than a stone and a half, to Red Rum, who himself was to carry top weight to those unmatched two victories and two seconds over the next four years. But forget mathematics, the huge Australian was trying to do it the only way he knew how, to blitz his opponents from the front. That might be fine over two miles – Crisp was the Champion Chase winner at Cheltenham – but how could he possibly last over Aintree's four and a half?

The die was cast at the sixth fence, Becher's Brook. Meeting it on a perfect stride, Crisp soared out and clear, and for the remaining 24 fences he and Richard Pitman never saw another horse. What happened for the next seven minutes would all but blow the mind and break the heart. Crisp treated the legendary Aintree fences with a disdain never seen before or since. On and on he sailed, a distant black shape a hundred yards clear, the 37 other runners just specks in his wake. He had run them absolutely ragged but, as he came up towards the grandstand, he had already completed two and a quarter miles. For him that should be race over. Now a whole extra circuit lay ahead.

That's when the enormity of Richard Pitman's problem began to grip the throat. Richard had been one of my best friends in the weighing room. We had travelled

The 1973 Grand National

by Brough Scott

The moment when Red Rum began his career as the ultimate Aintree hero

together, sweated together, been stretchered off together. Now he was having the most brilliant ride ever seen at Aintree. But he was a passenger on a champion going at two-mile pace. Come the finish, win or lose, he was going to be on a horse emptied of every drop of juice.

Tommy Stack was standing beside me. Four years later he would share Red Rum's epic fifth and final National. Now he was an injured, awe-inspired spectator, but one also riddled with doubts. "Jesus," he said as we watched Crisp and Richard blazing away towards Becher's on the second circuit, "there's no way he can keep up that pace for so long."

But he did, he did; skipping round the Canal Turn, pinging Valentine's, rocking on relentlessly all the way to the Melling Road. The pursuers were all so distant that the only thought was to just how bad Crisp must be feeling inside. He must have built up the biggest oxygen debt in racing history. But there was still no outward sign. Perhaps, just this once, the impossible could happen. But then, at the second-last, it showed.

It wasn't much of a mistake. Just a moment of awkwardness, but there was no doubting the split second of stagger as exhaustion clawed for a hold. Crisp and Richard were still clear and galloping relentlessly towards the last. But you knew the tanks were flashing empty. It was a long haul home.

2
Red Rum and Crisp

GRAND NATIONAL, AINTREE, MARCH 31, 1973

1. Red Rum 9-1jf
2. Crisp 9-1jf
3. L'Escargot 11-1

Winning Owner: Noel Le Mare
Trainer: Ginger McCain
Jockey: Brian Fletcher
Distance: ¾l, 25l
Also ran: Rouge Autumn (5th), Hurricane Rock (6th), Proud Tarquin (7th), Prophecy (8th), Endless Folly (9th), Black Secret (10th), Petruchio's Son, The Pooka, Great Noise, Green Plover, Sunny Lad (pu), Go-Pontinental (pu), Mill Door (pu), Grey Sombrero (f, dead), Glenkiln (f), Beggar's Way (f), Ashville (f), Tarquin Bid (f), Richeleau (f), Charley Winking (f), Proud Percy (f), Culla Hill (f), Canharis (bd), Beau Parc (pu), Rough Silk (pu), Princess Camilla (ref), Rampsman (pu), Nereo (pu), General Symons (pu), Highland Seal (pu), Mr Vimy (f), Astbury (pu), Fortune Bay (f), Swan-Shot (ref). 38 ran.

Red Rum (left) catches Crisp in the shadow of the post

Press Association

The eyes went back to the pursuers. Leading the pack was a white-nose-banded bay trained on the sands at nearby Southport by a second-hand car dealer called Ginger McCain. Red Rum had been both trained and ridden by Tommy Stack in his younger days. On National eve, Tommy had told me that for all Red Rum's sizzling five-win streak since joining Ginger, he thought his old partner, whose first visit to Aintree had been when dead-heating for a two-year-old seller on his debut under Paul Cook in 1967, would be "too clever" for Liverpool's demands.

On Red Rum, 25-year-old Brian Fletcher already knew different. Red Rum's cunning, his ability to look for landing space while still in mid-air, was to make him the most successful Aintree jumper in history. Crisp might be more than a distance clear, but Red Rum always saved something. And Brian – implacable, sometimes contrary Brian – never gave up hope.

Over the last and on towards us up that pitiless dog-legged 494-yard run-in, Crisp still had a full hundred yards of advantage. He was still galloping, Richard was still pumping. If they could just keep pushing, the huge black car that was Crisp would roll on over the line.

But we knew it was desperate. We shouted for Richard and the voice beside me shouted loudest of all. Jenny Pitman was always a frustrated spectator and watching

The dream had become a nightmare; it died only in the very shadow of the post

her husband's chance of ultimate glory brought extra, even to her fog-shattering voice. "Riiiiiiichard, Riiiiiiiichard," she screamed. Was that the tipping edge?

Down on the run-in, Richard, in extremis, pulled out his whip, cracked Crisp hard on the quarters, and in one fatal moment the game was gone.

Crisp rolled left away from the whip and, much, much worse, away from the line of the open run-in that skirts the Chair fence. Richard pulled him back on course but now all vestige of momentum drained away.

They got to the last railed 100 yards before the finish, but this was much more rocking horse than racer. It was terrible to watch. Fifty yards out and they were still clear but Red Rum was swooping. The dream had become a nightmare. It died only in the very shadow of the post.

It was a race like no other. History made it even grander with Red Rum and Ginger McCain returning the National to its status as British sport's No.1 event.

Yet the postscript always has to be the sight of that huge sweat-flecked black Australian horse staggering, hocks buckling, into the second enclosure in 1973. Red Rum became a legend, but it was Crisp's immortality in defeat that made this the greatest day of all.

red rum and crisp what they said

Ginger McCain, Red Rum's trainer

I remember watching the race from the top of the trainers' stand and thinking, as Red Rum jumped the second Canal Turn, 'great, we're going to be in the frame'. At the same time, I thought how unlucky it was to meet Crisp on a day like this. Then it became obvious that, fence by fence, we were pegging Crisp back a bit.

Even so, I was never confident we were going to win it until the final 50 yards. I watched the replay a number of times and I still wasn't sure we were going to get there!

After the race, everybody was talking about Crisp, Crisp, Crisp and, even though I like to think of myself as a sportsman, I'm glad we beat him. I've no regrets about that whatsoever. He ran a brilliant race but, whatever people said about Crisp, the record books say that Red Rum won it.

What goes on after you win the National was all a bit much to cope with that first time. It was all very strange to us and it's true to say we were taken off our legs a bit. I remember thinking that if I was ever lucky enough to win it again, I'd relish it a bit more – and 12 months later, we were back again.

To win what is, for me, *the* race, was amazing. I went to my first National when I was eight or nine and I can honestly say that even if the old lad had finished sixth or seventh that day it would have been the highlight of my training career. To win was very, very special indeed.

Richard Pitman, Crisp's jockey

I still remember every blade of grass in that race. Crisp was a bold, front-running type, and a hard puller, and going into the Grand National I thought we had an excellent chance. The decision was made to make the running and try to slow the pace from the front, even though Crisp always accelerated into his fences, like he was attacking them.

I remember that everything changed for us at the second-last. Crisp started to feel like a car with a flat tyre. His legs started to go sideways and he was suddenly so bottomed even his ears went lower.

On the run-in I made a basic error and hit him right-handed. He moved left away from the whip and it was enough to lose his momentum. I think that made the difference between winning and losing, not the weight he carried.

I could hear the snorting as Red Rum got near and I heard the drumming of his hooves. Crisp felt it too and, even though he was out on his feet, he tightened for a few seconds to try again. But he was just too tired.

To think I was going to win the National and then have the rug pulled from under my feet was a huge deflation. But that feeling only lasted a few moments – after I'd pulled up I was just elated at what a great ride I'd had. It's such a shame that people only ever remember how Crisp looked staggering up the run-in and not how fleet-footed he was over all those fences.

The 1975
King
George

by **Tony
Morris**

Instituted in 1951, the King George VI and

Queen Elizabeth Stakes has rapidly established itself as Britain's most important weight-for-age race – and as the midsummer European championship event. In its first 24 years, the roll of honour includes such great performers as Tulyar, Pinza, Ribot, Ballymoss, Right Royal, Ragusa, Busted, Park Top, Nijinsky, Mill Reef, Brigadier Gerard and Dahlia, the last-named having become the first dual winner when victorious in each of the last two seasons.

Those are hard acts to follow, but on paper at least the silver anniversary edition reads as though it might be something special; the fact Dahlia is an easy-to-back third favourite for her hat-trick bid indicates as much. She ran away from subsequent Arc hero Rheingold in '73 and cantered all over dual Classic-winning filly Highclere in '74, so why wouldn't she do something similar in '75?

The answer is not in Dahlia's four defeats this year. She did not peak until the summer in either of the two previous seasons, and then became devastating. And her most recent effort, in the Grand Prix de Saint-Cloud, showed that she is returning to form. No, the reasons why the five-year-old Dahlia does not capture the public's imagination this time are a three-year-old and a four-year-old who have been exceptional this summer.

The young gun Grundy, trained by Peter Walwyn, comes to Ascot after three Classic triumphs – in the Irish 2,000 Guineas, the Derby and the Irish Derby. And he has won them all so impressively that it seems he will start at odds-on.

The silver anniversary edition reads as though it might be something special

That is surely insulting to the no-less-admirable Bustino, who was the best of his age – and a St Leger winner – last year, and who, on his return at Epsom last month, smashed the mile-and-a-half course record.

They say that the weights at Ascot – a stone difference between three-year-olds and their seniors – is inclined to favour the youngsters, but nobody is handing this prize to Grundy on a plate, least of all Bustino's trainer Dick Hern, who has a strategy for success that worked famously on the same course back in 1949.

The Hern plan is an emulation of the one that enabled Alycidon to triumph over Black Tarquin in the Gold Cup – the employment of two pacemakers with the task of draining the last drop of stamina from the hot favourite. What Stockbridge and Benny Lynch achieved for Alycidon, Highest and Kinglet are now asked to achieve for Bustino.

Why wouldn't that work? After all, Bustino is a solid stayer, proven over a longer trip, while Grundy is a son of miler Great Nephew, and his grand-dam is by the sprinter Princely Gift. If Grundy has a weakness in the stamina department, the West Ilsley trio will surely find him out.

Yes, this could be a vintage renewal, so find a good pitch high up on the stand and prepare to watch the drama unfold.

Grundy's a flashy sort, to be sure, with his bright chestnut coat and his flaxen mane and tail, but you can forget the old horseman's lore about that type's generally being soft; he's proved he's tough, and he looks businesslike enough today as he

Gerry and Mark Cranham

Grundy (near side) finally gets the measure of brave Bustino

3

Grundy v Bustino

KING GEORGE VI AND QUEEN ELIZABETH DIAMOND STAKES, ASCOT, JULY 26, 1975

1. Grundy 4-5f
2. Bustino 4-1
3. Dahlia 6-1

Winning Owner: Dr Carlo Vittadini
Trainer: Peter Walwyn
Jockey: Pat Eddery
Distance: ½l, 5l
Also ran: On My Way (4th), Card King (5th), Ashmore (6th), Dibidale (7th), Libra's Rib (8th), Star Appeal (9th), Kinglet (10th), Highest (last). 11 ran.

passes by with young Pat Eddery aboard. Bustino's different, a solid, rangy bay, and a true professional. Joe Mercer, for so long the supreme stylist in the saddle, has him beautifully relaxed in his canter to post.

Was there ever any doubt about whose colours would show in front first? Hardly, given that Lady Beaverbrook owns all three of the West Ilsley runners, but blow me down if that's not Bustino leading the way, having made the faster break.

Not for long, though. Frankie Durr has Highest stoked up, and Eric Eldin is pushing Kinglet into contention. Mercer need not have worried, if indeed he had. When they settle down – if you can call that furious gallop settling down – Highest is striding clear, Kinglet sitting second, Bustino in third. Star Appeal is in pursuit of the Beaverbrook trio, and Grundy is not far behind.

Highest does his job well, but he couldn't last more than five furlongs at that pace. Now it's down to Kinglet to keep the momentum going, and so he does for a while, but Star Appeal has got ahead of Bustino, and there's no indication that Grundy is feeling the strain.

Kinglet is not man enough for the job. He is an ordinary staying handicapper and, having run the fastest mile of his life, he retreats. Mercer was no doubt hoping Kinglet would give him a lead as far as the turn for home, but that can't happen now, and he has to punch Bustino clear.

When he does that, it seems decisive. There's no let-up in the pace, so Grundy hasn't got his breather, and as they come into the straight, he's four lengths adrift.

These are champions, giving their all – a dead-heat is the only fair result

At least he's now second, because Star Appeal has weakened, but he's not gaining an inch on the free-galloping leader.

And yet, think how fast Bustino has gone. Is it possible his tank may run dry over those energy-sapping final furlongs? No sooner does the thought occur, and it becomes fact. Eddery's vigorous efforts are drawing Grundy closer, and Mercer is suddenly aware that danger looms.

At the furlong pole, the principals are neck and neck, and the advantage surely lies with the challenger. That chestnut nose shows just in front, but Bustino fights back and the issue is still in doubt.

Which to cheer for? Who cares? These are champions, giving their mighty all, and a dead-heat is the only fair result. But that's not to be, because in the final 50 yards Grundy edges ahead, passes the post a half-length to the good. Misty-eyed, you hug your neighbour, and ask the question to which you know the answer: "Wasn't that the greatest race you've ever seen?"

You're still in awe of what you've been privileged to witness when the time is announced. Grundy has broken the course record by almost two and a half seconds. Even Dahlia has cracked it, though finishing five lengths behind Bustino.

You know and appreciate immediately what those two heroes have done in providing you with the race of your life. But it will be some weeks before you realise at what cost to themselves, Grundy proving a shadow of his former self at York, Bustino breaking down before he could race again. They had run their hearts out for us.

grundy v bustino what they said

Peter Walwyn, Grundy's trainer

The build-up to the King George had been immense but I don't recall being particularly nervous. The biggest worry for a trainer is attempting to win a race with a bad horse!

Our day at Ascot had begun in the best possible fashion when the Grundy colours of Dr Vittadini were carried to success by his daughter Franca in the race for lady jockeys. By the end of that afternoon we'd saddled three winners.

The King George, as everyone knows, was quite a race. Dick Hern ran two pacemakers for Bustino as some people reckoned Grundy wouldn't stay. The pair set a fierce gallop, and then, with half a mile to run, Joe Mercer took Bustino to the front and went for home. They must have gone three or four lengths clear, and Pat Eddery was hard at work on Grundy. When our horse narrowed the gap, Bustino would pull out a little more. At the furlong pole Grundy drew level, but Bustino fought back. Grundy battled and battled to win by half a length. Two incredibly brave horses.

I was stunned. I suspect most people at Ascot that day felt much the same. Dick was the first to congratulate me. He shook my hand with the grip of a bear. The Queen presented the trophies. It was the perfect day. We celebrated that night with a dip in the new pool at Seven Barrows. Pat and his brother-in-law Terry Ellis joined the party. Grundy was a champion at two and three; that doesn't happen too often these days.

Joe Mercer, Bustino's jockey

Going into the race I really thought Bustino had a tremendous chance. There were some very good horses in the race, but he was such a tough horse; he had terrific pace and a tremendous cruising speed.

We planned to run three pacemakers because we knew the faster the race went the better it would be for us. In the end Riboson didn't run, which was a pity because he would have led us further than the other two pacemakers, probably into the final turn, where Bustino would have taken it up. Frankie Durr led us first on Highest, then Eric Eldin took it up on Kinglet. The two pacemakers did the job well for the first mile, but then I had to take it up half a mile out.

I think Bustino was left in front too soon, and if Riboson had run the result could have been different. Grundy was a very good horse, the winner of two Derbys, but it's very difficult to give away a stone in July and, were it not for the weight-for-age allowance, we would have beaten him.

We gave Bustino a canter five days later and he was dead lame with a tendon injury. In the race he changed legs a furlong from home and came off the fence and I think he must have injured himself then. It was such a shame he couldn't run again.

It's funny, but at the time you don't think, "this is one of the best races of the century". But Bustino was such a talented horse and Dick Hern had a very high opinion of him. I wish we had one like him now!

The Derby winner surrendered his lead to

the French Derby winner, and so the story of the race seemed told. But there then flashed a meteorite. A blur of speed. Dancing Brave. His body was slung low, his legs grabbed at the ground.

How enlightening, how riveting, if present-day technology had been available down the years for us to study speedsensing figures for that final furlong and a half at Longchamp. Did any Arc winner ever cover the same stretch of Paris grass at such a velocity?

By unleashing his pulsating late scythe, Britain's champion flicked asunder the best field assembled during the 1980s for a Prix de l'Arc de Triomphe.

Shamefully, due to incompetence, or perhaps more likely over-zealous patriotism, there's no video footage available for us to appreciate the colt's full, graceful sweep. Only the memory of those present at Longchamp can serve to narrate what happened in its glory.

They witnessed the scene the television coverage had missed. The French director had focused on the homeland's prime hope Bering, who'd snatched what appeared a decisive lead from Shahrastani – which may have briefly thrilled the director's compatriots, but there's no question viewers were being deceived with false hope.

For in the closing stages it was Dancing Brave who'd shot across the screen. He'd come and gone in a blink. He seemed to be travelling twice as fast as the opposition.

Dancing Brave seemed to be travelling twice as fast as the opposition

He delivered a charge so searing, so sensational, that Pat Eddery was shaking with exhilaration as he was led in by the groom to the winner's enclosure. Like the rest of us at Longchamp on that perfect Indian summer day, the jockey was in a state of disbelief. He was wide-eyed. We were wide-eyed. More than one of the more senior members of the crowd remarked it was a performance similar to Sea-Bird's 1965 Derby.

From somewhere, Prince Khalid Abdullah's colt had unleashed the explosive rush of a sprinter. For those fortunate to witness the event, the memory has become indestructible. Rarely for an Arc, there were no hard-luck stories. Instead, all parties, all represented nations, united in salute to a champion.

Eddery had won the previous season's Arc on Rainbow Quest. He was to win the following year's on Trempolino. Yet, talented as they were, neither generated the same degree of thrill.

He appreciated that the rivals Dancing Brave had left in his slipstream lacked nothing in proven excellence. They included Bering, who'd broken the French Derby record at Chantilly; Triptych, that most diligent of mares who never missed a headline dance, and, of course, Shahrastani, the colt who'd benefited from Greville Starkey's timing miscalculation on Dancing Brave at Epsom, but who'd then fortified the form with a win in the Irish Derby. For good measure, toss into the mix Shardari, the best older horse in Europe, and Acatenango, the German Derby winner.

Throughout most of the race, Dancing Brave was nearer to the rear and, at halfway, looked unlikely to improve on his position. In the circumstances, no doubt a few of

Gerry and Mark Cranham

**Dancing Brave (no.12)
flashes past Bering (no.14)
to claim the Arc**

4
Dancing Brave's Arc

LONGCHAMP, OCTOBER 5, 1986

1. Dancing Brave 11-10f
2. Bering 11-4
3. Triptych 64-1

Winning Owner: Khalid Abdullah
Trainer: Guy Harwood
Jockey: Pat Eddery
Distance: 1½l, ½l
Also ran: Shahrastani (4th), Shardari (5th), Darara (6th), Acatenango (7th), Mersey (8th), Saint Estephe (9th), Dihistan (10th), Iades (11th), Baby Turk (12th), Nemain (13th), Sirius Symboli (14th), Maria Fumata (last). 15 ran.

his followers lowered their binoculars with a resigned sigh that, yes, his season had been a long one, and this was a challenge too many.

At the front, the lead had swapped four times. Two furlongs from home, we witnessed a rarity – a trio, all carrying the colours of the Aga Khan, headed the field in line abreast. They were Shardari, Darara and, of course, Shahrastani.

Little more than a neck behind this large smudge of green with red trimmings came Triptych and Acatenango, and there, closing quickly on their outside, was Gary Moore on Bering. Shahrastani briefly seized the lead, but was soon cut down as Bering, who had always been in the preferred 'Arc' position, continued his charge.

For the first time in a furlong or two, we spotted Abdullah's green and pink. Eddery appeared on the outside with plenty to do. Perhaps too much to do. Two taps of the whip and whoooooosh . . . Dancing Brave took off.

No more fears of a race too many. He scythed down Bering in just a few strides and victory was sealed. Dancing Brave had gone by Bering with no more than half a furlong to the winning line, yet he'd won by a length and a half. Later, Bering's jockey said he couldn't believe the speed of Dancing Brave. During the debrief in the paddock, he looked as surprised as Eddery.

The win was rightful justice for Dancing Brave. Like astronaut Jim Lovell – "Houston, we've had a problem" – on Apollo 13's hapless mission to the moon, his fame until then had unjustly derived from a failure rather than his career

Dancing Brave scythed down Bering in just a few strides and victory was sealed

achievements on other missions. How wickedly unfair it would be to a colt worthy of mention in the same breath as Nijinsky and Mill Reef to be primarily remembered as victim of a bungled Derby ride.

On that day in Paris, to the immense credit of Guy Harwood and his team in Sussex, he'd looked in superb shape as he paraded in the paddock – this despite a taxing season where no challenge was ducked. It had stretched back to April and the Craven Stakes, where he'd started favourite on the strength of two relatively minor wins in the fading weeks of his juvenile season.

So he rolled into Longchamp with just the Derby defeat staining the record. After the Craven had come the 2,000 Guineas. After Epsom had come the Eclipse, then the King George, where he'd gone off 6-4 second favourite to Shahrastani (11-10), and was to leave no doubt as to who was the master of this generation.

As is the norm for an Arc prep, there followed a brief late-summer recess before he popped up the road to Goodwood for a Group 3, where he scared off opposition to such an extent that no SP was recorded. In the countdown to the first Sunday in October, the smoke signals lifting from camp Pulborough were unusually positive. Few were in doubt the colt would do battle in Paris at the peak of his powers. And so it proved.

The 1986 Arc will not only be remembered as a great race. But a race won with the greatest of elegance.

dancing brave's arc what they said

Guy Harwood, Dancing Brave's trainer

I had taken a flight to Paris on the morning of the race and had an early lunch by the Seine. It was one of those glorious Indian summer days. This was a fiercely competitive Arc with eight other Group 1 winners in opposition, but I remember a feeling of overwhelming confidence. We had Dancing Brave in better shape than any other horse in my life. The preparation had gone according to plan. The ground was perfect.

My one second of concern came two furlongs from home when I couldn't pick out the horse. I thought 'Pat, what are you doing to me?' Then, all of a sudden they were there, with that stunning burst of speed. It was almost like an explosion.

In motoring terms, it was similar to looking in the rear-view mirror and seeing nothing, then taking another glance half a second later and seeing a police car on your tail.

Like most champions, Dancing Brave raced low to the ground when at full speed. He was sweeping by the field with that impressive long stride of his.

After all the tension of the build-up and thrill over the result, all I wanted to do was collapse in a heap. Anyway, there was no time for a celebration because I was booked on a flight to Dublin for the sales the next day. I don't think we ever did have a party.

Even now, there wouldn't be too many days when I don't think about the horse. I've pictures of him everywhere about the house.

Criquette Head-Maarek, Bering's trainer

I have very fond memories of Bering: he was a real family affair, as he was bred by my father, ran in my mother's colours and was trained by me.

A very easy horse to train, he was a very nice individual, physically very impressive. He was the best middle-distance colt I've ever trained – I won the Prix du Jockey-Club with him and the track record is still his.

Even though he was beaten in the Arc de Triomphe, he put up a fantastic effort when it is considered that he chipped a knee in the race and must have run the latter stages on three legs. You could see his head went up and it was as if something was hurting him, but he ran a great race and would have won if we had not been unlucky to come up against a champion like Dancing Brave.

Bering didn't like to come second – he was the boss of my string and even led them up the training gallops!

Great races are full of emotion. They bring

nervous, impatient waiting, eager wanting, hope, fear, anticipation, anguish, debate. The 1986 Cheltenham Gold Cup was riddled with emotion, awash with adrenalin. Spectators and participants were drained, for Dawn Run's victory was one of racing's great, suspenseful moments.

There are the actors and actresses, and there is the stage. In 1986, both were extraordinary and, on a fine March day, they came together for a unique performance. It was one of those days that all who were there will always remember.

Twenty years ago, there was an even greater sense of an Irish gauntlet thrown down each March, a challenge where victories and defeats mattered in the edgy friction between the British and Irish nations. Dawn Run, more than any champion since Arkle, was Ireland's horse, and every Irish man and woman had a small right to claim her, proudly, passionately, as their own. Dawn Run was for Ireland.

So, fiercely, was her owner, Charmian Hill. An Irish patriot with a feisty, awkward, opinionated spirit in a diminutive body, Hill was never going to be merely a signer of cheques. Sixty-one when she bought the three-year-old Deep Run filly at the 1981 Ballsbridge Sales for 5,800gns, Hill was clutching a letter refusing a renewal of her rider's licence when she won a bumper on Dawn Run at Tralee the following June.

Part of what rouses a crowd is the history that comes to a race. Dawn Run brought a lot of history, woven around Hill and the Mullins family. Unlike Dawn Run's trainer,

Dawn Run, more than any champion since Arkle, was Ireland's horse

Paddy Mullins, Hill was not a quiet, tolerant soul but a horsewoman with views, especially views about jockeys. She had views about Tony Mullins, Paddy's son, the jockey who rode Dawn Run more times than anyone else, and won on her more times.

When Dawn Run appeared in the 1983 Sun Alliance Novices' Hurdle at Cheltenham, Hill believed that Mullins, then 21, was too young and inexperienced for the task. Ron Barry, an Irishman in Britain, replaced him. "I would never employ an English jockey," said Hill. Dawn Run finished runner-up to Sabin du Loir.

Mullins was restored to the saddle until a trip to Ascot in November. This time his replacement was a different Irishman, the talismanic Jonjo O'Neill. "It's no disgrace to lose the ride to someone as good as Jonjo," said Mullins, with dignity and generosity.

Universally known as Jonjo, O'Neill, twice champion jump jockey, could drive hard as well as skilfully in the saddle, and charm with a twinkling smile and wry lilt out of it. People loved Jonjo.

In 1984, the new combination won the Irish and English Champion Hurdles. Then, with Jonjo injured, Mullins won the Sandeman Aintree Hurdle and Grande Course de Haies d'Auteuil, the French Champion Hurdle. It was a unique and remarkable achievement, not least because the Grande Course de Haies was over different obstacles, over three miles one and a half furlongs. Dawn Run was a versatile as well as gutsy champion, the only horse ever to land the treble of Champion Hurdles.

Gerry and Mark Cranham

Wayward Lad leads Forgive'n Forget (left) away from the last, with Dawn Run (black cap) and Run And Skip in pursuit

5
Dawn Run makes history

CHELTENHAM GOLD CUP, MARCH 13, 1986

1. Dawn Run 15-8f

2. Wayward Lad 8-1

3. Forgive'n Forget 7-2

Winning Owner: Charmian Hill
Trainer: Paddy Mullins
Jockey: Jonjo O'Neill
Distance: 1l, 2½l
Also ran: Run And Skip (4th), Righthand Man (5th), Observe (last), Combs Ditch (co), Earls Brig (f), Von Trappe (f), Castle Andrea (pu), Cybrandian (pu). 11 ran.

Jumping fences presented a different test. Fast and flat over hurdles, with a distaste for being organised, Dawn Run was not a natural jumper of fences. When Hill told Paddy Mullins she wanted the target to be the Cheltenham Gold Cup, Mullins was uneasy.

In November 1984, at Navan, Dawn Run made a winning debut over fences, ridden by Tony Mullins, but a leg injury then kept her off the track for more than a year. In December 1985, Dawn Run returned to win at Punchestown and Leopardstown but in January, sent to experience Cheltenham, she reached the open ditch at the top of the hill and unseated Mullins.

Hill was not impressed. Jonjo was booked for the Gold Cup but fierce weather scuppered plans for another prep race. When O'Neill schooled Dawn Run, he emerged believing that the mare did not like jumping fences. That was one of the teasing ingredients of the 1986 Gold Cup. The horse that was supported with the fiercest passion, the 15-8 favourite, was having only her fifth race over fences, and she looked like a hurdler.

Wayward Lad, in contrast, was a wonderfully athletic, smooth, accurate jumper, three times winner of the King George VI Chase, with a different fear for his admirers. He didn't really stay three and a quarter miles.

There was no such doubt about John Spearing's Run And Skip, who had improved into an exciting front-running stayer, leading all the way to win both the Welsh

As Wayward Lad faltered, O'Neill conjured a spine-tingling, thrusting rally

National and the Anthony Mildmay, Peter Cazalet Memorial Chase. Forgive'n Forget had won the previous year's Gold Cup for Jimmy FitzGerald, while David Elsworth's Combs Ditch had only just been beaten by Wayward Lad in the King George.

Dawn Run, who had never raced over as long a trip before, duelled for the lead with Run And Skip, both mixing good jumps with bad. After a bad mistake at the water, and a worse one at the top of the hill, five from home, Dawn Run fell back and came under strong pressure. Attention switched elsewhere, to the strong-travelling Wayward Lad and Forgive'n Forget.

O'Neill, at his most powerful, forced Dawn Run back into the battle and, with a great leap two out, back into a narrow lead. It was quickly wrested from her, as Wayward Lad and Forgive'n Forget quickened ahead.

At the last, there was little between the pair, with Dawn Run landing third and Run And Skip still at their heels but, as they set off up the telling hill, Wayward Lad and Graham Bradley forged on, two lengths clear. Then, suddenly, as Wayward Lad faltered, O'Neill conjured a spine-tingling, thrusting rally from Dawn Run. With the crowd delirious, she nosed ahead to become the only horse ever to win both the Champion Hurdle and the Gold Cup, the latter in a course record time.

In a hat-trampling stampede, Charmian Hill was carried aloft and so, after he had weighed in, was Jonjo O'Neill, who hoisted Tony Mullins onto his own shoulders.

It was a unique occasion – a race for memories, but one with a sad aftermath. Three months later, at Auteuil, ridden by Michel Chirol, Dawn Run fell and was killed.

dawn run makes history what they said

Jonjo O'Neill, Dawn Run's jockey

This was a day I will never forget, a magical day. The whole of Ireland knew Dawn Run would win and the way it happened made it more exciting than ever.

I remember every blade of grass we covered. We went a cracking gallop with Run And Skip and Cybrandian in the race. I was always trying to get a breather into Dawn Run but I couldn't.

She missed the water and Run And Skip passed us. Then he cut across us, which kind of disappointed her. I had to pull out wide to get round at the next fence, which he missed and I pinged. We went down the hill hammer and tongs but I had Wayward Lad and Forgive'n Forget breathing down my neck.

I thought if we pinged the second-last the others would have no chance. She did ping it but Run And Skip, 'Brad' on Wayward Lad and Mark Dwyer on Forgive'n Forget went past us as though we were standing still.

I thought that as she seemed beaten now I might as well get that breather into her. She relaxed, got her breath and then picked up like a motorbike. She flew the last. I could see the boys trying their best but the race was hers.

I can still hear the roars and shouts and see the hats flying. It's so easy to remember days like that. It was just a magic moment.

Graham Bradley, Wayward Lad's jockey

Wayward Lad was a very good horse, the winner of three King Georges, but he never quite got the trip at Cheltenham. He was at his best on a flatter track like Kempton, but he was an absolute superstar of a horse.

The race came a couple of years after the introduction of the 5lb allowance for mares, and although Dawn Run was a very good horse, the allowance has to have helped her.

Throughout the race Wayward Lad travelled very well and jumped brilliantly. He was getting a bit lazy in his old age, though, and I had to put him under pressure a bit running to the last. We jumped the last in front and I really thought we would win it. Halfway up the hill, two lengths up, I thought it was our turn at last, but then Wayward Lad just ran out of petrol and the mare beat us by a length. You can tell it was a great race as we broke the track record.

I've never heard noise like it after Dawn Run won, the roars and the cheering. Everyone just got swept up in the emotion of it all, and it was just fantastic. I can't say anything better than it was an unbelievable privilege to ride in that race. It was the best-quality race I ever rode in, with some of the best horses ever involved in a Gold Cup.

The 1964 Cheltenham Gold Cup was a

defining moment in racing history, involving two great horses, each carrying the hopes of a nation, with the supreme champion emerging victorious.

In a race that fully lived up to its huge build-up, Arkle, Ireland's rising star, served notice for the first time that he was the greatest steeplechaser who ever lived by dethroning Mill House, Britain's reigning champion.

The seven-year-olds had both triumphed at the Cheltenham Festival 12 months before. Arkle proved himself the champion novice by cantering away with the Broadway (now Royal & SunAlliance) Chase by 20 lengths, and two days later Mill House was hailed as the best young chaser since Golden Miller when winning the Gold Cup by 12 lengths.

They met for the first time in the Hennessy Gold Cup at Newbury in November 1963, when the Fulke Walwyn-trained Mill House gave 5lb to Tom Dreaper's Arkle and beat him just over eight lengths into third place.

Most pundits accepted that result as a fair reflection of their merits, without realising that Arkle had a genuine excuse. He had jumped the third-last well, only to slither in the mud on landing, thus losing much of his momentum. Nor could anyone have predicted that he had so much improvement in him.

The Hennessy result, and Arkle's mishap, meant that the two camps on either side of the Irish Sea were optimistic in the run-up to the eagerly anticipated rematch in the Gold Cup, especially as the principals were unbeaten in the interim. Mill

Arkle served notice that he was the greatest steeplechaser who ever lived

House won the King George VI and Gainsborough Chases, and Arkle's three victories included the Thyestes and Leopardstown Chases. Both seemed to have the jumping world at their feet.

The England v Ireland rivalry had extra edge because Walwyn had beaten Dreaper into second place in the two previous Gold Cups, with Mandarin and Mill House both proving too good for Fortria.

Mill House started at odds of 8-13 for a Gold Cup double, with Arkle at 7-4. They scared away all but two rivals in the only renewal of the race to be run on a Saturday since 1947. One rival was Pas Seul, winner of the Gold Cup in 1960 and a great champion at his best, but now a light of other days; the other was King's Nephew, conqueror of Mill House the previous season and now fresh from a triumph under top weight in the Great Yorkshire Chase. Neither made any impact on the proceedings. There was a snow flurry just before the race, but the sun was shining and visibility was perfect when the flag fell.

Mill House went straight into the lead and stayed there for three miles. Arkle was soon in second place, but he pulled hard in the early stages and gave Pat Taaffe an uncomfortable ride for a while.

Neither horse made a significant mistake, and the race started in earnest when Arkle, who had never allowed the gap to grow to more than four lengths, moved closer on the downhill run to the third-last. The two were both going strongly at the penultimate fence, which Mill House jumped on the inside fractionally in front, but on the home

Empics / Topham Picturepoint

Arkle has the race in safe keeping as he takes the final fence ahead of Mill House

6
Arkle v Mill House

CHELTENHAM GOLD CUP, MARCH 7, 1964

1. Arkle 7-4
2. Mill House 8-13f
3. Pas Seul 50-1

Winning Owner: Anne Duchess of Westminster
Trainer: Tom Dreaper
Jockey: Pat Taaffe
Distance: 5l, 25l
Also ran: King's Nephew (4th). 4 ran.

turn Willie Robinson began to use the whip on him. The response was generous but inadequate, and the issue was settled in a matter of strides.

With Taaffe also employing the whip, though sparingly, Arkle jumped the final fence a length in front and, showing a turn of speed that his rival lacked, galloped up the hill full of running to score by five lengths in a stunning display of sheer class. Pas Seul was 25 lengths behind in third.

Peter O'Sullevan said at the climax of his BBC commentary: "Arkle going away now from Mill House. This is the champion, this is the best we've seen for a long time, Arkle is the winner of the Gold Cup ... I have never heard such cheers from the stands at Cheltenham as Arkle proves himself the champion chaser in the British Isles."

Taaffe said: "I knew we had it won three fences out, when I was still behind." Many years later his owner, Anne Duchess of Westminster, was asked which was the greatest of Arkle's victories, and she replied: "The first Cheltenham Gold Cup, when he beat Mill House – it was so exciting."

In no race has the mantle of supremacy passed from one great champion to another more decisively, and 'Himself' was mobbed as he returned to the winner's enclosure – by British fans as well as Irish, for greatness transcends national loyalties. Fulke Walwyn was thunderstruck – not surprisingly, as his paragon had lost despite running the race of his life.

This was the first of four meetings the pair had after their initial Hennessy clash, and on each occasion Arkle took handsome revenge. In the 1964 Hennessy,

"I have never heard such cheers from the stands at Cheltenham. . ."

he made nearly all the running and beat Mill House (received 3lb) by 28 lengths into fourth place. In the 1965 Gold Cup he led from start to finish and cantered home 20 lengths clear of his rival.

Their last encounter came in the Gallaher Gold Cup at Sandown in November 1965. Arkle conceded 16lb to Mill House and beat him by 24 lengths into third place, shattering both the latter's course record and any hope that the 'Big Horse' could ever regain his title.

Strictly on form, Arkle's win in the 1964 Gold Cup would have made him the greatest steeplechaser ever seen up to that point (replacing Easter Hero) even if he had never run again. Little did any of us realise that his performance graph was still on a steep upward curve that in the next two years would take him into realms previously undreamt of.

Superlatives became inadequate as, in majestic, swaggering, ruthless style, he easily defied 12st in the Irish Grand National and 12st 7lb in the Hennessy (twice), Whitbread and other handicaps, taking the glory that had seemed destined for Mill House. He displayed outstanding pace, stamina, jumping ability and courage under crushing burdens, never falling and always giving his best.

Had Arkle not been injured in his prime, he would have eclipsed Golden Miller's record of five Gold Cup victories, but that would merely have altered the wording of his story, not its magnitude. The 1964 Cheltenham Gold Cup defies the laws of perspective: the further it recedes into history, the greater it appears.

arkle v mill house what they said

Johnny Lumley, Arkle's groom

I remember the overwhelming tension. It started to build from the moment I arrived at Arkle's box at 8am. From then on every minute to the race dragged like an hour. After months – it really was months – of banter between the Irish and British, this was crunch time.

Pat Taaffe had convinced me we'd win. I'd had on a month's wages, about £40, at 15-8. But this wasn't a money thing. It was about pride. In the Railway Hotel the night before, a chap of about 16st insisted that even if he rode Mill House they'd beat Arkle.

It was a bitter day with flurries of snow and I was shaking, possibly due more to nerves than the cold, as I prepared Arkle for the race. I fussed over him. He had to look at his best. As I led him up in the paddock, Pat again insisted we'd win.

The course had a different configuration then, and the best place for the groom to watch was down at the final fence. Mill House made the running, tracked by Arkle. Three fences out I saw Willie Robinson go for his whip. My confidence soared. From that point our horse was always travelling the better.

As I led him in, the Irish went crazy with joy. Hats were flying in the air and people didn't bother about catching them. I was walking across a carpet of trilbies. That night I went back to the Railway Hotel – is it there still? – to celebrate. Unfortunately, most of the British who'd been staying there had made their way home. I didn't bother going to bed that night.

Willie Robinson, Mill House's jockey

Having beaten Arkle in the Hennessy I naturally hoped I would beat him again, but he had done fantastic things in the meantime and he obviously had to be reckoned with.

I went straight to the front and Pat Taaffe was sitting on my heels with Arkle pulling hard. After jumping the water, Pat joined me and going up the hill he said: "What way are you going?" He meant how well was I going, so I told him: "I can't answer you that until we come down off the hill but I'm all right at the moment."

"I'm the same," Pat said.

We came down the hill very fast and, when we straightened up for the second-last, Mill House started to run flat. The spark had gone and there was no response for the whip, which I later dropped. But that made no difference – he was a horse you didn't have to hit.

It was a big disappointment to be beaten like that. I had always thought that there was never going to be more than heads and necks between them, and if Arkle was going to beat us he would only just do so.

Still, people have often said that Mill House was never the same again because he was disheartened by Arkle, but I don't think there's any question of that. He actually developed leg and back trouble.

Racing too often draws on war for metaphor.

It is an easy allusion to make, but it is too often unsuitable. While epic battles end with the degradation of one side or another, the best races result in the ennoblement of both.

A case in point is the Irish Champion Stakes of 2001. The meeting between Fantastic Light and Galileo at Leopardstown that September afternoon elevated both horses in status, irrespective of who passed the post in front.

It was a spectacle born out of the competitive nature of the thoroughbred. That would hardly distinguish it from the other races in this series, however, and, in truth, there were other elements critical to its composition as a highly theatrical event.

Like all good drama it had context. Fantastic Light and Galileo had already met in the King George at Ascot, with victory going to the latter. However, while the winner had skimmed the rail all the way, Fantastic Light had been forced to cover extra ground around weakening horses on the home turn. Moreover, in so doing he had expended vital energy in a rapid burst, leaving him with little in reserve for the finish.

In the circumstances, the two lengths that Galileo had over his rival at the finish looked flattering, and a rematch between the pair at Leopardstown was sure to

The 2001
Irish
Champion

by **James
Willoughby**

Like all good drama, it had context – a rematch was sure to be a close-run thing

be a close-run thing. And that wasn't the only reason to expect something special.

Twelve months previously, the Irish Champion Stakes had staged a precursor to this latest clash between Godolphin and Ballydoyle superstars. On that occasion, an artful use of pacemakers by the Aidan O'Brien stable had seen Giant's Causeway get through along the inside rail to win, while the Saeed Bin Suroor-trained Best Of The Bests was forced wide and finished only third.

This time both concerns were fielding pacemakers; Give The Slip for Godolphin and Ice Dancer for Ballydoyle. Their use – and misuse – was to prove pivotal to the outcome.

Whatever anticipation had accumulated around the race soon intensified when the stalls banged open. The inexperienced Paul Scallan rousted Ice Dancer with such urgency that he took off into a clear lead, soon absenting himself from the race as a tactical entity.

Fortunately for Godolphin, Give The Slip's experienced pilot Richard Hills wanted no part of this unproductive scenario, and he calmly allowed his mount the opportunity to fulfil a carefully ordained role. Approaching the home turn, Give The Slip was guided off the rails and allowed the stalking Fantastic Light and Frankie Dettori the precious opportunity to charge up the inside.

So roles were reversed from the previous year. This time it was the Ballydoyle runner who was forced into covering extra ground, and the position of the home turn

George Selwyn

Galileo (left) and Fantastic Light give everything in the gruelling final furlong at Leopardstown

7
Fantastic Light v Galileo, #2

IRISH CHAMPION STAKES, LEOPARDSTOWN, SEPTEMBER 8, 2001

1. Fantastic Light 9-4
2. Galileo 4-11f
3. Bach 20-1

Winning Owner: Godolphin
Trainer: Saeed Bin Suroor
Jockey: Frankie Dettori
Distance: hd, 6l
Also ran: Give The Slip (4th), Ice Dancer (5th), Siringas (6th), Chimes At Midnight (last). 7 ran.

at Leopardstown in the hottest part of the race magnified the advantage. It was immediately evident to the onlooker that Galileo would have a massive task in trying to run Fantastic Light down.

In the face of such a well-conceived plan, Mick Kinane on Galileo was rendered helpless. Watching the video again, it really does seem that he was prepared for the *coup de grâce*, but there was little that he could do.

The events of the home turn mirrored a game of chess, in which sound tactical positioning during the opening leads to a killer move deep into the game. As soon as Dettori had claimed a favourable pitch behind his pacemaker, the strategic advantage was bound to accrue to Fantastic Light.

Responding to the urgency of his plight, Kinane threw Galileo into pursuit. His mount came barrelling off the apex of the bend with such vigour that he elicited a huge roar from the crowd. Galileo even managed to get almost upsides inside the final furlong, but Fantastic Light had sufficient momentum to hold him by a head under a strong, right-handed drive.

The final furlong was played out to such rapturous support from the partisan crowd that it seemed there was the danger of anticlimax at the imminent acknowledgement that their champion had been defeated. True to the reputation that the love of horses runs deep in the Irish psyche, however, both horses were given a hearty reception as they trooped into the winner's enclosure.

The final furlong played out to rapturous support from the partisan crowd

The depth of the encounter was not lost on either Dettori or Kinane, who, in the light of their vast experience, could reasonably be assumed to have become inured to such occasions. Both described the experience of being involved in such an epic contest in glowing terms, drawing attention to the unwavering determination of their mounts in a drawn-out finish.

Dettori summed it up thus in his recent autobiography: "I'd done my job to the best of my ability, but if the horse doesn't want to do it too you are wasting your time. You have to give the credit to Fantastic Light, who was a hero that day."

As ever, the reaction of the public provided the best testimony of the lasting impact of the race. There were many letters to the *Racing Post* from readers simply overjoyed to have been affected by such a moving occasion. And many said that the defeated Galileo had only enhanced his reputation in their eyes.

"Galileo has epitomised everything that is good and exciting about racing," wrote Jonathan Hoar from Poole. "If Frankie Dettori had not ridden the race of his life, he would still be unbeaten."

The Irish Champion Stakes was not a war. It was a stunning fusion of two natural forces in a wholly artificial context; it was something for us to celebrate because we had the idea; it was as good as it gets; it was a horserace.

fantastic light v galileo, #2 what they said

Frankie Dettori, Fantastic Light's jockey

My game plan was to stalk Galileo, then pull out inside the final furlong and nail him on the line. The evening before the race I discussed tactics with Sheikh Mohammed and Sheikh Maktoum. They wanted me to jump out in front and steal first run. I thought it madness, but my argument fell on deaf ears.

There was no late change of mind from the boss – thank goodness! It helped that Richard Hills, who rode a blinder on our pacemaker Give The Slip, agreed to stay a little off the rail, so I had a choice of passing him inside or outside.

Ice Dancer, a 200-1 outsider, took us along at a spanking pace, but Richard essentially controlled the race in second, with me tracking him, and Galileo behind us. As the pacemakers weakened, I dived through on the inner with just under two to run. When I saw Galileo arrive on our outside, I thought we were beaten.

We hooked up for the last two furlongs, two great champions racing head to head, nostril to nostril – a bit like that famous duel between Seabiscuit and War Admiral.

Fantastic Light was just too brave for Galileo. He relished the battle more and, when Galileo couldn't get past him, it broke his heart. I knew we'd won, but I was so drained mentally and physically that I didn't have the strength to punch the air.

Mick Kinane, Galileo's jockey

It was always going to be tough because Galileo was coming back from a mile and a half. The pace was very fast and I settled my horse in fourth, just behind Frankie, who made his move as we turned in when his pacemaker came off the rails to let him through.

In some ways it was a bit like the previous year when I got the run through on the inner on Giant's Causeway and Frankie on Best Of The Bests had to go round our pacemaker. This time I had to go round Richard Hills on Give The Slip but with about 100 yards to race I honestly thought we were going to get there. Galileo responded coming up the straight, he was digging deep and catching Fantastic Light.

Then my horse changed his legs and for some reason his stride began to shorten near the finish. At the line we were beaten a head. Obviously it wasn't the result I wanted but it was a great race between two exceptional horses; a great race and great for racing.

Anyone who wonders why jumping exercises

the pull that it does over so many enthusiasts should watch the 1984 Whitbread Gold Cup. And then they should watch it again, and again, until they appreciate what a fantastic race it was, and what a marvellous tale it told.

What more can you ask for than to have three horses separated by two short heads at the end of three miles five furlongs and 24 fences, culminating in victory for the sport's most popular owner, Queen Elizabeth the Queen Mother?

For that is what we had with Special Cargo getting up in the very last stride to win by a whisker from Lettoch, with his stablemate Diamond Edge, already twice a winner of the race, the same distance away in third. It was breathtaking stuff and no wonder the usual huge Sandown crowd cheered its head off.

So much more added to the tale, not least the fact that both Special Cargo and Diamond Edge were examples of their trainer Fulke Walwyn's brilliance in bringing horses back from long injury absences.

Special Cargo's career had begun in 1978/79 when he won three of his six starts, but problems loomed the following season when he was unplaced in three attempts and did not appear after December 8.

The following season went much better with three more wins, but he was not able to start his 1981/82 campaign until January, and before the end of February it was all over.

The 1984
Whitbread
Gold Cup

by **George
Ennor**

Three horses separated by two short heads after three miles five furlongs

For a long time it must have looked as if it *was* all over – for good. Special Cargo's injuries were so serious that almost two years elapsed before he was able to run again – he was off the track from February 20, 1982 to February 10, 1984 – but the combination of training and veterinary expertise and the patience of all involved were handsomely rewarded.

Special Cargo won three of five starts before the Whitbread, including Sandown's Grand Military Gold Cup – which he was to win twice more – and a further race at the Esher venue, demonstrating his liking for the track.

It was a sunny spring afternoon on Whitbread day 1984, and 13 horses lined up for the big prize. Plundering, who had beaten Special Cargo into fifth place at Cheltenham 17 days earlier, was 7-2 joint-favourite with Ashley House, one of the Dickinson 'Famous Five' in the previous year's Gold Cup but without a win all season, although he had been second in Plundering's Cheltenham race.

Next in the betting were Diamond Edge, who had won the Whitbread in 1979 and 1981, and Lettoch, who had begun the season as a novice and in his first run over fences had beaten none other than subsequent Gold Cup winner Forgive'n Forget in a novice chase at Stratford.

Special Cargo was the only other trading in single figures, at 8-1, and the reason Diamond Edge was preferred to him was partly due to the fact that stable jockey Bill Smith, whose last ride this was, chose to ride him, leaving Kevin Mooney to come in for the ride on Special Cargo. Victory for either would be a seventh Whitbread for their trainer.

Gerry and Mark Cranham

Plundering has the call on the run-in but Diamond Edge (partly obscured) and Special Cargo (left) are about to throw down the gauntlet

8
Special Cargo's Whitbread

WHITBREAD GOLD CUP, SANDOWN, APRIL 18, 1984

1. Special Cargo 8-1
2. Lettoch 11-2
3. Diamond Edge 11-2

Winning Owner: Queen Elizabeth the Queen Mother
Trainer: Fulke Walwyn
Jockey: Kevin Mooney
Distance: sh hd, sh hd
Also ran: Plundering (4th), Skegby (5th), Kudos (6th), Fortina's Express (7th), Ashley House (8th), Sointulla Boy (9th), Integration (last), Ocean Cruise (pu), Polar Express (ur), Donegal Prince (f). 13 ran.

The outcome of the race could also have a major bearing on the trainers' title, which was being fought out by Michael Dickinson and Fred Winter. Dickinson ran Ashley House and Lettoch, while Winter's hopes rested with Plundering, and victory for any of that trio would virtually clinch the championship, even though there was more than a month of the season to go.

Special Cargo wasted no time in demonstrating his wellbeing as he led over the first three fences. At the third, the downhill fence going away from the stands, came the first drama as Donegal Prince fell and Lettoch and Robert Earnshaw performed some amazing acrobatics to avoid being brought down. The fact that Lettoch was beaten only a short head after losing what Timeform reckoned to have been a dozen lengths in the incident, makes you wonder how he would have fared without this near-disaster.

Starting down the back straight, Diamond Edge took up the running, making light of his 13 years as the oldest runner in the race and jumping with great enthusiasm as he showed the way to a group including Ashley House, rank outsider Polar Express, Special Cargo and Plundering.

A circuit later, it all looked like proving a bit much for the royal horse as he was struggling to keep tabs on the leaders and, by the end of the back straight, victory looked unlikely, to say the least.

If it hadn't happened, you would have said it was unbelievable

Diamond Edge still led over the last of the Railway fences, but by the time they reached the Pond fence, Lettoch had taken over in front as Plundering challenged. Special Cargo was under strong pressure and his cause seemed lost.

Over the last, Plundering led by a whisker from Lettoch, with Diamond Edge a couple of lengths back and Special Cargo two more lengths adrift of him – closer than he had been at the Pond fence, but still with a formidable task ahead of him.

Starting on the run to the line, Lettoch regained the lead from Plundering as Diamond Edge challenged and, with almost all eyes focusing on this part of the action, it came as something of a surprise as Special Cargo forced his way back into the picture over on the far side.

Lettoch and Diamond Edge were going hammer and tongs for the post with neither giving an inch, but Special Cargo was finishing with such gusto that, having been almost written off three furlongs earlier, he nailed the other two right on the line for as dramatic a victory as the Whitbread had known in its 27-year history.

It was thrilling enough by any standards, a race that no-one who saw it will ever forget. Two short heads and the Queen Mother as the winning owner – it was the sort of stuff that takes your breath away.

Luckily the Sandown spectators had enough left in their lungs to give horse, owner, trainer and jockey (to say nothing of the pair so narrowly beaten) the reception they deserved.

If it hadn't happened, you would have said it was unbelievable.

special cargo's whitbread what they said

Kevin Mooney, Special Cargo's jockey

My proudest moment. I feel so privileged to have ridden the Queen Mother's biggest winner. There was no pressure on me because in their final two pieces of serious work, Special Cargo was beaten 20 lengths by Diamond Edge. In truth, he wasn't in the same furlong.

Sandown had been baked by a burning sun and the ground was too fast for Special Cargo. The others were always going a stride too quick. However, he started to pick up at the Pond fence, and although rather getting under the next, he began to close on the three in front, one of whom was Diamond Edge.

Special Cargo flew the last, changed his legs, then took off. He finished so fast I was confident he'd won. For the only time in my career, I gave a salute as we crossed the line.

Diamond Edge's jockey Bill Smith, who was having his final ride, was the first to reach over to shake my hand. I was invited to the royal box, where the Queen Mother said that after such a great four-horse finish, it was a shame there had to be three losers.

It had become a tradition for Saxon House's big-race winners to be toasted by all involved at the Malt Shovel pub, near the stables. It was a grand party. Later that year, I was invited to the Queen Mother's celebration at Clarence House.

The one sadness about that Whitbread was the fact the first four horses broke down on the ground.

Bill Smith, Diamond Edge's jockey

Of all the greatest races, I think this was the greatest training performance. Both the winner and my horse were old crocks with legs like eggshells, but Fulke Walwyn was an old master at patching them up and training them for the big day.

The decision to ride Diamond Edge was really made easier because of the ground. Special Cargo, who had been the 500th winner of my career earlier that season, was never beaten at Sandown but he needed soft ground. Diamond Edge loved the top of the ground and the going was very fast that day. He was really a Gold Cup horse, while Special Cargo was a good handicapper.

The race went just perfect for me. The horse jumped particularly well down the back and travelled well. We hit the front about 50 yards out and, looking back, I think I got there a fraction too soon. Throughout the last furlong I was just thinking 'can he hold on?' because he was running on fantastically well.

Afterwards we were all invited into the royal box to watch the re-run with the Queen Mother. She was such a wonderful lady and kept saying to me 'Oh, there you are!' as we watched, even though she owned the winner!

I always was a pretty bad loser, but just to be associated with that race was wonderful. Diamond Edge was first into the winner's enclosure and got such a tremendous cheer he thought he'd won!

Jay Gatsby was sure of it. "Can't repeat the

The 1990 Breeders' Cup Mile

by **Steve Dennis**

past?" he cried incredulously. "Why, of course you can!" The 51,000 crammed into Belmont Park on a sunny autumn afternoon would have given plenty for Gatsby's optimism, for the present was affording them little comfort.

The 1990 Breeders' Cup had been billed as the greatest show on earth, but halfway through the performance, the paying customers were stunned and sore of heart.

First they had watched Britain's star speedster Dayjur tear up the track to a barnstorming victory in the Sprint – or rather they almost had, as he hurdled a shadow 50 yards from the post and then again virtually on the line, gifting victory to Safely Kept. Then they witnessed the duel of the season between superstar distaffers Bayakoa and Go For Wand, which was building into a legendary conclusion until Go For Wand's leg snapped like a twig halfway up the stretch and she fell flailing into the dirt. She couldn't be saved and, so it seemed, neither could anything be salvaged from the afternoon.

Then, out into the tumult of Belmont came the runners for the Mile, the first of them an Irish colt ridden by a 54-year-old man who had just spent five years in retirement, including a year in prison.

Lester Piggott had returned to the saddle just 12 days earlier and now here he was, riding the favourite. It seemed just like old times.

Piggott, the darling of the punters and the ice-cream sellers and the former scourge of the racing establishment, had drawn stumps on his phenomenal career five years earlier, bowing out with a final-day win aboard Full Choke at Nottingham.

Now here Lester Piggott was, riding the favourite . . . it seemed just like old times

A brief training career, which included victory in the Oaks d'Italia and the Coventry Stakes at Royal Ascot, ensued before the mightiest rider of the age fell victim to his own avarice and served 12 months of a three-year sentence for failing to pay sufficient income tax. Piggott was lost off the saddle. So he came back.

He reapplied for his licence and drew thousands to Leicester on his first day back when he had three rides, finishing a short-head runner-up on the first of them, Lupescu. Next day he was back in the winner's enclosure aboard Nicholas, trained by his wife Susan, at Chepstow. The following week he went to The Curragh to ride four horses for his old genius-in-arms Vincent O'Brien, who had been instrumental in encouraging him to reapply for a licence. All four won. Thought you had seen it all before? Well, there's some news for you.

Now, owing to an injury sustained by Royal Academy's regular partner John Reid in a fall at Longchamp three weeks earlier, Piggott was resplendent in the green, gold and white silks of Classic Thoroughbreds plc – a syndicate set up by O'Brien and another great friend and ally, Robert Sangster – to ride Royal Academy, trained like so many of Piggott's great winners by O'Brien, in the Mile.

Royal Academy might have been better off in the Sprint, but the presence of the burly bullet Dayjur had led connections to seek a softer target. The Irish 2,000 Guineas runner-up had turned in his best display of the year when beating Great Commotion in the July Cup, but Dayjur had left him for dust in the Ladbroke Sprint Cup at

S. Kikkawa

Lester Piggott checks the winning distance on Royal Academy (near side) over Itsallgreektome on the rail

9
Lester and Royal Academy

BREEDERS' CUP MILE, BELMONT PARK, OCTOBER 27, 1990

1. Royal Academy 5-2f
2. Itsallgreektome 36-1
3. Priolo 9-2

Winning Owner: Classic Thoroughbreds plc
Trainer: Vincent O'Brien
Jockey: Lester Piggott
Distance: nk, ¾l
Also ran: Steinlen (4th), Expensive Decision (5th), Who's To Pay (6th), Markofdistinction (7th), Lady Winner (8th), Jalaajel (9th), Go Dutch (10th), Shot Gun Scott (11th), Great Normand (12th), Colway Rally (last). 13 ran.

Haydock. He wasn't entitled to be favourite on form, but the potency of nostalgia led his price to contract and he was market leader when the stalls opened.

Ranged against him were the cream of the world's turf milers, with the previous year's winner, the Wayne Lukas-trained Steinlen, in the vanguard. From Britain came Frankie Dettori's mount Markofdistinction, the Queen Elizabeth II Stakes winner, and Distant Relative, sunk in that QEII but winner of the Sussex Stakes and the Prix du Moulin. France sent Prix Jacques le Marois winner Priolo, lightly raced and heavily backed.

Royal Academy missed the break, by design, as Piggott dropped him in behind and bided his time. As the field swung for home, Royal Academy faltered and Piggott had to gather him together and send him on again, though now there were seven horses in front of him on the short run-in.

The outsider Itsallgreektome, under Corey Nakatani, was making the best of his way home on the rail, and with less than a quarter of a mile to run, Piggott produced Royal Academy to challenge and the pair came rolling down the outside, rolling back the years.

The years out of the saddle, and in truth the years themselves, had taken their toll. Piggott might have lost a little of his agility, a little of his style, a little of his finesse, but some things you never lose and he had lost nothing of his racing brain. He may not have been perched so impossibly high in the saddle but he timed his

Some things you never lose and Piggott had lost nothing of his racing brain

final thrust as if he had never been away, as if he had never grown old.

Royal Academy, ostensibly a non-stayer but carried along on the tide like the thousands in the stands, was brought immaculately to lead in the last 20 yards, and when the camera clicked he was a neck in front of Itsallgreektome, with the running-on Priolo third and Steinlen fourth.

Those who had seen all Piggott's 29 Classic wins and more than 4,000 successes were left shaking their heads, as the ghost from the past had come galloping by and replayed all their memories in one irresistible stretch run. Those who hadn't, had read the papers and were as jawdroppingly thrilled as the rest. There was bedlam at Belmont. It was one of the greatest sporting comebacks of all time, more so because it knitted together the past and the present so adroitly.

Royal Academy was a son of the mighty Nijinsky; memories of other Piggott/O'Brien heroes such as Sir Ivor, Roberto, The Minstrel and Alleged were fresh once again. Those days had gone forever, we thought. But, now, for a few minutes ...

Gatsby would have raised his glass in delight. It seemed that you could indeed repeat the past. But as Lester Piggott came trotting back towards the stands on Royal Academy, those eyes not too misty to focus would have seen something quite unprecedented, something new that underlined the fact that here was something truly special, an event that raised the sport to a higher level.

Piggott's face, described in his heyday as having all the emotional output of a well-kept grave, was wreathed in smiles.

lester and royal academy what they said

Lester Piggott, Royal Academy's jockey

I didn't start riding again until October, and after that it all came back so quickly. Royal Academy was originally going to run at Newmarket in the week before the Breeders' Cup and someone else had been booked to ride him, but Vincent changed his mind because the horse was going so well at home that he decided to take him to America.

Royal Academy was a lot like Nijinsky really – a big horse, he used to get on his toes a bit. I sat on him for the first time only two days before the race.

In the race, when the stalls opened he was a little bit slow, although that wasn't a bad thing because they went very fast until halfway, after which I was able to get into a good position to pick them up.

Just before we straightened up, I was going terribly well, following Markofdistinction. But something happened – I don't know if he stepped in a hole, but whatever it was, he lost all his momentum, like he had been shot.

It took him another 50 yards to pick up again and I had to really ride him hard from then onwards to the finish, but he responded.

I always thought I was just going to get up in the straight and he stuck on well. It was unbelievable – it meant so much to everybody.

Lester Piggott was speaking on his video My 12 Greatest Races,
released in 1991 by Castle Vision

Vincent O'Brien, Royal Academy's trainer

The Breeders' Cup Mile had always been in the back of my mind as an ideal race for Royal Academy, as he was probably a seven-furlong horse, and I think you need that sprinter's pace to be able to travel well in the early part of a race like that.

After John Reid's injury, Lester approached me at Newmarket sales looking for the ride, and I was only too pleased to put him up, especially as Royal Academy was the perfect ride for Lester – a hold-up horse whose head had to be dropped in front on the line.

The preparations went well – the horse travelled alone on a specially chartered plane on the Thursday, walked out on the Friday and had a canter under Lester on the morning of the race.

The race itself went according to the script – Lester dropped him out and was able to manoeuvre wide turning in. At that point the horse seemed to stumble, for no apparent reason, but not much momentum was lost and he hit the front with 100 yards to go, exactly as instructed – probably the only time Lester did what he was told.

Is there a time when you officially become

an old git? Hard to quantify, perhaps, but in racing terms at least, it's a fair bet that you have earned the status when you start droning on about golden ages, those ambrosial days of yore when every aspect of the Turf was so entirely superior (and spectacles were rose-tinted).

It can become tiresome. Best Mate's fans must be heartily fed up at the contempt with which those who revere Arkle dismiss their modern-day champion, while anyone who exalts Istabraq has doubtless heard more than enough unflattering comparisons between the triple Champion Hurdle winner and a list of names who never did quite what their hero did at Cheltenham.

Then again, those who look back to the 1970s to identify hurdling's nonpareils can point to some compelling pieces of evidence. Golden age or whatever, they were quite a bunch, a richly talented group whose very names are evocative of a series of hotly contested hurdling championships that spilled out at both ends of the decade, from Persian War to Sea Pigeon.

The latter formed one third, alongside Night Nurse and Monksfield, of the peerless triumvirate who came to the fore in the mid-1970s and have cast the longest of shadows ever since. Three of the best-loved jumpers we have ever seen, they were each of them enormously talented, each massive public favourites. Between them, they dominated the hurdling scene for six years, starting with Night Nurse's Champion Hurdle success in 1976, thereby reducing to bit players a supporting cast who were top-grade performers in their own right, chief among them lovable rogue Birds Nest.

The 1977
Templegate
Hurdle

by Nicholas
Godfrey

Golden age or whatever, they were quite a bunch, a richly talented group

Night Nurse's second victory, in 1977, has been described as the highest-quality hurdle race ever run and there, with Sea Pigeon only fourth, the winner's superiority over second-placed Monksfield was two lengths. However, a last-flight error had contributed to the runner-up's defeat in the Champion, whence a fierce Anglo-Irish rivalry was born, Yorkshire versus County Meath, rival camps that were to come face to face only 17 days later at Aintree in an epoch-making encounter. With Sea Pigeon absent, it was left to Night Nurse and Monksfield to produce the most unforgettable contest of an unforgettable era.

Night Nurse was the leading light of Peter Easterby's powerful Malton string (Sea Pigeon was a stablemate). The ultimate professional, this indefatigable gelding was a bold front-runner, sharp at his hurdles, amazingly consistent and, by the time he reached Aintree in April 1977 – a couple of unexpected mid-season defeats notwithstanding – holder of a relentless record of achievement that testified to his supremacy over the division. Easterby, who described Night Nurse as "hard and brave", explained: "What made him so special was that he was a natural jumper, brilliant from the first time we schooled him."

Then there was Monksfield, little 'Monkey', the entire small in stature but massive in heart who emerged from humble beginnings at the little-known stable of Des McDonogh in Ireland. Monksfield possessed a rare fighting spirit, the spirit of the

Empics / Alpha

Monksfield (left) and Night Nurse fly the final flight together before sharing the spoils in a scintillating finish

10
Night Nurse and Monksfield

TEMPLEGATE HURDLE, AINTREE, APRIL 2, 1977

=**1.** Night Nurse 4-5f
=**1.** Monksfield 7-2
3. Peterhof 10-1

Winning Owner: Reg Spencer (Night Nurse), Michael Mangan (Monksfield)
Trainer: Peter Easterby (Night Nurse), Des McDonogh (Monksfield)
Jockey: Paddy Broderick (Night Nurse), Dessie Hughes (Monksfield)
Distances: dead-heat, 15l
Also ran: True Song (4th), Cooch Behar (5th), Straight Row (6th), Flying Diplomat (7th), King Neptune (8th), Fighting Kate (9th), Magic Note (ref). 10 ran.

street fighter who relished a punch-up. He got plenty of those over the years, being subjected to some fearsome beatings from his riders in those less whip-conscious days.

It seems scarcely credible now, but on the day Red Rum claimed his third National, we were treated to two great contests for the price of one, two races destined to go down in the annals of racing history. Even if Red Rum stole the headlines in the aftermath, not for nothing has this two-mile-five-and-a-half-furlong contest been voted the greatest hurdle of all time in this poll.

Although a field of ten went to post – including Peterhof, who had beaten Monksfield in the previous year's Triumph – the race looked a classic head-to-head. The betting agreed: it was 4-5 Night Nurse, who had to give 6lb to his rival, sent off a 7-2 chance. It was 8-1 bar.

Night Nurse's supporters could look back at Cheltenham for evidence of a decisive verdict over the Irish terrier, but it was a different story this time. Under regular partner Paddy Broderick, Night Nurse took up his customary position at the head of affairs, but his jumping was by no means as fluent as usual. Three out, he stood off too far and made an uncharacteristic blunder, landing virtually on top of the hurdle and letting Monksfield pass him.

What followed was an epic as the pair duelled up the Aintree straight. Both gave absolutely everything in an extended battle that lasted three furlongs, the last half of which – after another slight mistake two out from Night Nurse – involved both horses responding to the strongest driving from their riders. Picture it now:

Neither deserved to lose and, for once, neither did: the pair were inseparable

Broderick on Night Nurse, like a Victorian gentleman upright in the saddle, bringing down his whip both in front and behind the saddle; the frenetic Dessie Hughes – later to become Monksfield's regular jockey, but here deputising for the injured Tommy Kinane – throwing the lot at his valorous partner.

The latter just held the upper hand throughout this spirited match until Night Nurse, lion-heart intact despite his errors, clambered back in the final stride. Neither deserved to lose and, for once, neither did: the pair were inseparable, a dead-heat was called – and thankfully the stewards did not see fit to change things after an inquiry.

As John Randall, racing's foremost historian, suggested decades later, this was a "race of superlatives". He explained: "The most thrilling hurdle race of all time resulted in the most historic dead-heat and Night Nurse, in view of his weight concession, produced the greatest single performance by any hurdler in the history of the sport."

Timeform awarded Night Nurse a rating of 182, a mark that remains the highest ever given a hurdler. In *Chasers & Hurdlers 1976/77*, they said the clash had produced "as protracted and stirring a finish as that famous one between Grundy and Bustino".

Look at the DVD: you won't quibble – and both horses came back for more. Night Nurse, maybe never quite as good again, was still talented enough over fences to finish second in a Gold Cup; Monksfield won the next two Champion Hurdles.

They simply don't make 'em like that any more. Sometimes there is no point losing sleep over whether you're starting to sound like an old git.

night nurse and monksfield what they said

Paddy Broderick, Night Nurse's jockey

Night Nurse was the best hurdler of the last century and obviously the best I ever rode; he was just a brilliant horse, and it was wonderful to ride him.

During the Aintree race he was travelling brilliantly, making the running, until he made a terrible, bad mistake three out. He stood off too far and hit the top of the hurdle hard. He frightened the life out of himself and he didn't jump the next nearly as well as he should. He was nervy and looking at the hurdle after that, though normally he was a brilliant jumper.

I got him running again after the last and he just got back up to dead-heat. When you're going that fast it's impossible to tell who has won and I wasn't really sure if Night Nurse had got up or not.

Afterwards I was very disappointed because he would have won easily if he hadn't made that mistake. It didn't matter that he was carrying more weight, he would still have won if he hadn't hit the hurdle. He ran a great race over what was a much longer trip than the Champion Hurdle, and even though I was disappointed to only dead-heat with Monksfield, to get a finish like that in a race like that was just fantastic.

Dessie Hughes, Monksfield's rider

I hadn't been expecting to be riding Monksfield but Tommy Kinane, who was then his regular jockey, was injured just before Aintree and I was offered the mount, probably because I'd just won the Gold Cup on Davy Lad.

I was obviously thrilled to be on him but I knew that it was bound to be a tough race as he was always such a lazy horse.

Going to the third-last, we were still a few lengths behind Night Nurse, but I remember he missed the hurdle and that helped us to get on terms.

Monksfield, on the other hand, never made mistakes – he was tidy and no matter how he met a hurdle he would always come away from it running.

He was also a horse who always kept finding for you, which meant I was sure the long run from the last was going to suit me, and so I was pretty confident that we were going to get there.

Neither Paddy Broderick nor I knew which of us had won, and in the end I was pleased it was a dead-heat – when it's that close you always are.

You wouldn't be able to ride a horse these days in the way I rode Monksfield, but he responded every time I hit him. I was hard on him, but you had to be.

That was Monksfield – he was one of those horses who would stop if you put the whip down, but if you kept asking him for more, he would keep battling for you.

The greatest Grand National winner? There are

no arguments: Red Rum. Others ran more times, were placed more times, but none has claimed more first prizes in the hardest steeplechase contest in Britain, run over obstacles that present a fearsome test like no other jump course in the land that spawned the modern sport.

The greatest Grand National? That's open to debate, but 1977 must come near the very top of the list, primarily because it was the race in which Red Rum made history by winning the race for the third time and pulled together the strands of his Aintree career. He injured a foot less than a week before the 1978 running, for which he was clear ante-post favourite, and was retired.

Lifting the 1977 National out of that season's form book and judging it solely as an event, it was a notable race – after all, the top-weight won by 25 lengths, conceding 22lb to the runner-up – but perhaps not a great one. Forty-two runners set out, and a furious pace produced seven fallers at the first fence, the worst drop-out rate for 25 years. By the fence after Becher's on the first circuit, a further seven, including that year's Gold Cup winner Davy Lad, had exited, leaving just 28 standing.

Approaching Becher's on the second circuit, Andy Pandy, the favourite, was at least ten lengths clear and seemingly going away. He knuckled over, as did second-placed Nereo, who in turn hampered What A Buck. Red Rum was left in front.

This was the moment that greatness came into play, for jumping ability was the

Jumping ability was the magic key that unlocked the door for Red Rum

magic key that unlocked the door for Red Rum at Aintree. Compact and well-made, he was bred for the Flat, by a 2,000 Guineas runner-up out of a seven-furlong winner, by a sprinter. But breeding counted for little in the National. His careful jumping, boundless stamina, extreme courage and inbuilt adaptability were everything, and they came into their own when mixed with trainer Ginger McCain's meticulously timed preparation.

Superb jumping ability had to be highest among the attributes. How else could he have crossed 150 Grand National fences safely, with hardly a noticeable blemish, and been beaten by only two of the 180 horses who took him on?

In 1977, after he had been left in front sooner than jockey Tommy Stack would have liked, one more example that jumping counts double round Aintree was to come. Churchtown Boy, who had won the Topham Trophy only 48 hours previously, drew to within two lengths of Red Rum at the second-last fence, only to blunder.

Red Rum was foot-perfect there and at the last and, pushed out almost to the line, he drew clear as the cheers built to a climax with every step he took along the long, dog-legged run-in. Stack took his left hand from the reins a few strides from the finish, and gave Red Rum a mighty slap of congratulation.

For millions of television viewers, Peter O'Sullevan summed up the moment: "It's hats off and a tremendous reception. You've never heard one like it at Liverpool. Red Rum wins the National!"

Howard Wright

Press Association

Red Rum is out on his own as he comes up the run-in to a hero's welcome

11
Red Rum's third National

GRAND NATIONAL, AINTREE, APRIL 2, 1977

1. Red Rum 9-1
2. Churchtown Boy 20-1
3. Eyecatcher 18-1

Winning Owner: Noel Le Mare
Trainer: Ginger McCain
Jockey: Tommy Stack
Distance: 25l, 6l

A thunderous duel that climaxed in three horses

virtually inseparable as they crossed the line: the Breeders' Cup Turf of 2003 may well have been the most exciting race in the 20-year history of a series not exactly short on heartstopping contests.

Certainly, it is hard to envisage a more thrilling finish than the one played out in the Californian twilight at Santa Anita, in the shadow of the San Gabriel mountains.

First, though, the context. The Turf, run at a trip and on a surface that most top US-trained runners never try, habitually looks vulnerable to a top-class European performer. In 2003, there were three to choose from: Ballydoyle's dual Derby winner High Chaparral, bidding to follow up his success at Belmont Park in 2002, the Godolphin globetrotter Sulamani, fresh from a Grade 1 triumph, and Falbrav, described as the "best horse in the world" by his trainer Luca Cumani.

However, only two of them figured as Sulamani never looked at home on the fast ground. It didn't matter. High Chaparral and Falbrav produced a classic, with an unexpected late turn from another party. More of that later. High Chaparral and Falbrav had history, following the latter's controversial defeat in the Irish Champion Stakes. High Chaparral had got first run on Falbrav that day, with the latter, a bull of a horse, looking all dressed up with nowhere to go on the rail as his rival pounced.

Since that race, though, Falbrav had dropped down in trip to record an emphatic victory in the Queen Elizabeth II Stakes, while High Chaparral had disappointed in the Arc when third behind Dalakhani.

High Chaparral and Falbrav produced a classic, with an unexpected late turn

The combination of tight turns and fast ground gave rise to hopes that Falbrav's suspect stamina would last out, and when Darryll Holland kicked on two furlongs out – making sure *he* got first run this time – he looked the likely winner.

What followed in the stretch was pulsating indeed. Falbrav barrelled ahead with High Chaparral under strong pressure to close. Falbrav, always terrifically hard to pass, gave everything, but it was his misfortune to be up against a tremendously resolute opponent in High Chaparral, who responded to Mick Kinane's fierce drive on his outside with a valorous effort. Half a furlong from the wire, High Chaparral finally wore down Falbrav, only for an interloper to appear as if from nowhere on the outside in the shape of America's unheralded Johar, who flashed alongside High Chaparral on the line. It took 15 minutes before the verdict was announced: the first dead-heat in Breeders' Cup history.

Falbrav was just a head back in third, having added to his immense reputation in defeat. He went on to finish his career with another top-level success in Hong Kong, while High Chaparral headed to stud as a hero. And Johar, the horse who so nearly did for them both? He raced just once more, finishing 16th of 18 in the Japan Cup, before injury ended his career and denied him the chance to get rid of an unfortunate paradoxical legacy. He came out on top in a memorable clash of the titans – without ever achieving the status of 'titan' himself.

Nicholas Godfrey

AP Photo / Benoit Photo

Johar (far side) and High Chaparral are inseparable; Falbrav squeezes into the frame just behind

12

High Chaparral, Johar and Falbrav

BREEDERS' CUP TURF, SANTA ANITA, OCTOBER 25, 2003

=**1.** High Chaparral 11-2
=**1.** Johar 20-1
3. Falbrav 5-2

Winning Owner: Michael Tabor (High Chaparral), The Thoroughbred Corporation (Johar)
Trainer: Aidan O'Brien (High Chaparral), Richard Mandella (Johar)
Jockey: Mick Kinane (High Chaparral), Alex Solis (Johar)
Distance: dead-heat, hd

In the 1971 2,000 Guineas, the two greatest

contemporaries in racing history met for the only time and Brigadier Gerard, Britain's Horse of the Century, emerged victorious over Mill Reef.

For strength in depth, 1970 produced the best crop of two-year-olds ever seen in Britain and the champion, My Swallow, beat Mill Reef by a short head in the Prix Robert Papin en route to a clean sweep of the top French races. The Guineas was billed as a rematch between those two colts, who had both scored easily on their reappearance.

Brigadier Gerard, though unbeaten, was neglected in the build-up, partly because he had not run since the Middle Park Stakes, but his trainer, Dick Hern, was a master at getting a horse ready first time out. The field of six runners was the smallest for the race since 1888 but the others included Nijinsky's brother Minsky, champion two-year-old in Ireland and the Vincent O'Brien-Lester Piggott representative.

My Swallow led from the start and Geoff Lewis soon took Mill Reef over to track him in the centre of the course, with Brigadier Gerard a couple of lengths behind. The Brigadier was the first of them to come under pressure when given a slap with the whip two furlongs out, and the effect was immediate. In full flow running down the hill, he stormed ahead well over a furlong out and, continuing to respond to Joe Mercer's rhythmic driving, strode away up the final climb, despite drifting towards the stands' side, until at the line he was three lengths clear.

The Brigadier's dazzing display of sustained finishing speed

It was a dazzling display of sustained finishing speed and it thwarted Mill Reef, who would have triumphed in almost any other Guineas. That colt eventually won his duel with My Swallow by three-quarters of a length and might have finished closer if ridden with more restraint, but he would never have matched the winner at a mile. The tail-swishing Minsky was another five lengths away in fourth place.

John Hislop, the winner's owner-breeder, later wrote accurately: "It was the most impressive victory in the Two Thousand since Tudor Minstrel spreadeagled his opponents in 1947; moreover it was gained at the expense of two exceptional colts, without a semblance of a fluke."

In this and many subsequent races, Brigadier Gerard set the standard by which all later champions have been measured and found wanting. Beaten only once in 18 starts, he proved himself the greatest miler of all time and was also brilliant at longer trips. During his three seasons on the Turf, this ultimate product of British breeding became the embodiment of consistency, courage and sheer class.

Mill Reef improved over middle distances and was never beaten again, winning the Derby, Eclipse, King George and Arc in 1971, but he was laid low by a virus as a four-year-old and the much-anticipated rematch between the two great champions never took place.

The debate continues as to which of them was the better, but on the only occasion they met Brigadier Gerard was supreme.

John Randall

Central Press Photos

Brigadier Gerard (right) sweeps majestically away from Mill Reef (centre) and My Swallow (far left)

13
Brigadier Gerard v Mill Reef

2,000 GUINEAS, NEWMARKET, MAY 1, 1971

1. Brigadier Gerard 11-2
2. Mill Reef 6-4f
3. My Swallow 2-1

Winning Owner: Jean Hislop
Trainer: Dick Hern
Jockey: Joe Mercer
Distance: 3l, ¾l

Lester Piggott's amazing strength in a finish

enabled him to win many races that looked totally beyond him and there have been few better examples of his power than Roberto's Derby in 1972. "It would be difficult," wrote Timeform in their *Racehorses* annual, "to minimise the part Piggott played in making Roberto the winner."

They were right, although there was a bit more to it than that. Trained by Vincent O'Brien, Roberto had been the top two-year-old in Ireland the previous year and had begun his second season with a decisive success at Phoenix Park, which resulted in his starting second favourite for the 2,000 Guineas. Ridden by the Australian Bill Williamson, Roberto ran extremely well at Newmarket, making ground through the final furlong before being beaten just half a length by High Top, the pair clear.

Roberto's chance in the Derby appeared very obvious and he duly started 3-1 favourite against 21 opponents. Controversially, Piggott took over the ride from Williamson – despite the latter being passed fit following a fall 11 days before the Classic. Even though Williamson had been promised the jockey's percentage if Roberto won, this was by no means a popular move.

Piggott proved pivotal in Roberto's success, however. With two furlongs to run, the colt was one of three horses still in with a serious chance of Derby glory. The others were the front-running 50-1 chance Pentland Firth, Pat Eddery's first Derby ride, and Rheingold, whom Roberto was destined to engage in a dramatic duel.

A finish that has seldom been equalled on Flat racing's most prestigious stage

Having overcome trouble in running two furlongs out, Roberto challenged between his two rivals. Just as he started to do so, Rheingold hung to his left and Pentland Firth edged to his right, leaving Roberto as the meat in the sandwich. Piggott threw everything at his mount, but Rheingold seemed just to be holding his challenge until the final 25 yards, when four more sharp cracks from his rider's whip forced Roberto's nose in front on the line to win by a short head. Piggott's strength was decisive in a titanic struggle, while Roberto himself demonstrated enormous courage to respond to his rider's urgings.

In normal circumstances, a well-backed favourite winning the Derby under the country's most revered jockey after a thrilling finish would have been greeted with an ecstatic reception. Not this time, though. Thanks to the unpopular nature of the decision to jock off Williamson, polite applause was the order of the day.

This was in stark contrast to the cheers that greeted Williamson when he came back after riding Captive Dream to win the race that immediately followed the Derby. It wasn't an event of particular significance and it wasn't a particularly notable piece of riding, but it gave the spectators a chance to vent their feelings.

More than three decades later, however, it probably wasn't an affronted sense of sportsmanship that prompted *Racing Post* readers to vote for Roberto's Derby. It was the memory of a supreme effort from both horse and rider, and a finish that has seldom, if ever, been equalled on Flat racing's most prestigious stage.

George Ennor

14
Roberto and Lester Piggott

DERBY, EPSOM, JUNE 7, 1972

1. Roberto 3-1f
2. Rheingold 22-1
3. Pentland Firth 50-1

Winning Owner: John Galbreath
Trainer: Vincent O'Brien
Jockey: Lester Piggott
Distance: sh hd, 3l

**Roberto (right) pips
Rheingold on the line
after a memorable duel**

Empics

Choose your own superlative, but don't expect

to find one that truly does justice to Arazi's unforgettable performance at Churchill Downs. Reviewing the video nearly a decade and a half later, it remains a struggle to trust the evidence of one's own eyes. This was a display that beggared belief: put simply, Arazi looked a wonderhorse that day on the dirt, when he treated America's top juveniles with absolute contempt on their home patch.

Trained by French legend François Boutin, the little chestnut son of Blushing Groom had already earned a big reputation before he crossed the Atlantic, having won a handful of France's most prestigious two-year-old contests. After a comfortable success in the Grand Critérium, Arazi appeared so far ahead of his European contemporaries that his owner Allen Paulson, when asked if the colt was the best horse he had owned, was moved to respond: "He's the best anyone has ever owned!"

Paulson insisted on Arazi having the chance to live up to his billing. After he had sold a half-share to Sheikh Mohammed for a reported $5 million, the colt was sent to the Breeders' Cup, where no European-trained horse had previously managed even a place on the dirt (though Sheikh Albadou caused a major shock in winning the Sprint hours before Arazi took to the track).

An unfamiliar surface, a terrible draw (widest of all, 14 of 14), Europe's dismal record: Arazi may have been sent off favourite at just over 2-1, but the odds appeared stacked against him. When he made a tardy start under Pat Valenzuela, it looked

"Here indeed is a superstar," exclaimed the track caller. "Absolutely sensational!"

a case of yet another much-touted European having dirt kicked in his face.

Literally speaking, that did indeed happen, and Arazi looked uncomfortable with the kickback early on as leading domestic hope Bertrando set the pace. Entering the back straight, Arazi, still 15 lengths behind the leaders, had passed just one horse.

Then, when asked to quicken, Arazi went past his rivals as if they were petrified, going by them horse by horse on the inside, the outside, wherever Valenzuela sent him. Such was the dramatic nature of his back-stretch move that it would have been little surprise if, when he finally reached the leaders, he had had nothing else to give. Yet Arazi reached Bertrando two furlongs out and ran straight past him, powering away to leave both locals and visitors stunned by an electrifying performance. "Here indeed is a superstar!" exclaimed the track caller. "Absolutely sensational!"

As a result of that victory Arazi was the first horse to become champion juvenile in both Europe and the States – but after knee surgery he was never the same again. Although he won his seasonal debut at three at Saint-Cloud, he flopped in the 1992 Kentucky Derby, could win only a single Group 2 event thereafter, and had an undistinguished career at stud.

That Arazi lost his lustre is unarguable, but he had a lot of lustre to lose after that Breeders' Cup. Subsequent travails cannot diminish the memory of what was one of the most extraordinary displays in racing history. Seldom can a horse have left such a stupendous visual impression.

Nicholas Godfrey

Mirrorpix

Arazi walks on air as his outclassed rivals toil in the distance

15
Arazi the astonishing

BREEDERS' CUP JUVENILE, CHURCHILL DOWNS, NOVEMBER 2, 1991

1. Arazi 21-10f
2. Bertrando 5-2
3. Snappy Landing 61-1

Winning Owner: Allen Paulson and Sheikh Mohammed
Trainer: François Boutin
Jockey: Pat Valenzuela
Distance: 4¾l, 3½l

Judged on his victory in the Prix de l'Arc de

Triomphe of 1965, Sea-Bird may have been the greatest racehorse of all time, for he put up a performance of dazzling brilliance to crush the strongest international field ever assembled for one race.

Trained at Chantilly by Etienne Pollet, Sea-Bird was the only horse in living memory to win the Derby without coming off the bridle, and he had an afternoon stroll in the Grand Prix de Saint-Cloud before having three months off the course prior to his supreme test.

For strength in depth, the field for the 1965 Arc was unique. Sea-Bird's main rival was Reliance, a great horse in his own right and unbeaten winner of the Prix du Jockey-Club, Grand Prix de Paris and Prix Royal-Oak. The 20 runners from six countries also included Free Ride, the best older horse in Europe; Tom Rolfe, winner of the Preakness and champion three-year-old in America; Anilin, the best horse ever trained in Russia; Meadow Court, second to Sea-Bird in the Derby and winner of the Irish Derby and King George; and sundry other winners of races now designated Group 1. Sea-Bird was the 6-5 favourite.

Marco Visconti, from Italy, set the pace on the soft ground, with Anilin soon a close second and Sea-Bird lobbing along in sixth place. At the entrance to the straight Pat Glennon, Sea-Bird's Australian jockey, allowed him an extra inch of rein, and

For strength in depth, the field for the 1965 Arc was unique

the response was explosive; the colt surged past Marco Visconti and was clear in an instant. Reliance went in pursuit and, in a majestic display of class, left the rest of the star-studded field trailing in his wake, but he was himself humiliated by the supreme champion.

Sea-Bird drifted left into the centre of the course in the final furlong but, under hands-and-heels riding, galloped further and further ahead, and Glennon was patting him on the neck well before the line, which he reached six lengths clear. Reliance had five lengths to spare over Diatome, who came late to deprive his stablemate Free Ride of third place, with Anilin and Tom Rolfe next.

Bill Shoemaker, rider of Tom Rolfe, said: "I kept looking over at that big dude [Sea-Bird] and the jock had a double nelson on him. He was going so nicely that I said to myself, I'd better get out of the way because if that horse is ever turned loose he'll run over me."

The photo-finish print showed that the actual (rather than the official) margins were four and a half lengths and four, not six lengths and five, but the form was still sublime. Neither Sea-Bird nor Reliance ran again, but Diatome took the Washington DC International the following month.

Sea-Bird, beaten once as a juvenile and unraced as a mature horse, had rivals for the title Racehorse of the Century. But on the evidence of the 1965 Arc, none deserved it more.

John Randall

APRH

Sea-Bird comes right away from the best Arc field ever assembled

16
Sea-Bird's Arc

PRIX DE L'ARC DE TRIOMPHE, LONGCHAMP, OCTOBER 3, 1965

1. Sea-Bird 6-5f
2. Reliance 9-2
3. Diatome 15-2

Winning Owner: Jean Ternynck
Trainer: Etienne Pollet
Jockey: Pat Glennon
Distance: 6l, 5l

They could so easily have been under the

sod, not galloping joyfully to glory on top of it. In 1981, Bob Champion and Aldaniti came up the famous Grand National run-in in front, outdoing all the emotional stories turned up by the old race down the years and recording a scarcely credible success on the biggest stage of all.

As Timeform, in their typically restrained way, noted later, the result was a "triumph over adversity" for both Champion and Aldaniti. Less than two years earlier, Champion had been in a hospital bed after being diagnosed with testicular cancer. He had begun the arduous and painful process of chemotherapy which would eventually restore him to health, but his spirits were understandably at rock bottom.

One of the few things keeping him going was news of the progress of Aldaniti, in training with Josh Gifford, Champion's main employer. Unfortunately, the news was not particularly good. In November, Aldaniti broke down, for the third time, and had to spend virtually the whole of the following year convalescing. Champion and Aldaniti made a right pair.

A year passed, and the health of both improved slowly. Champion made his comeback in the summer of 1980 and was soon among the winners. Aldaniti was on his way back too, and in February 1981 was reunited with Champion for the Whitbread Trial Chase at Ascot. After 15 months on the sidelines it was just nice to see them together on the racecourse again; their 14-1 victory was a bonus that delighted all who witnessed it. Next stop was the big one: the Grand National.

For two who had overcome so much, there was nothing to fear from 30 fences

The comeback kids were sent off second favourite for the great race, and for two who had overcome so much there was nothing to fear from the 30 fences or their 38 rivals. They had both come so far; four and a half miles more would surely not stop them now.

Aldaniti took to the big fences almost immediately – a blunder at the first concentrated his mind admirably – and by the 11th fence his bright white face was at the head of affairs. Turning back towards the stands for the final time, he had the 1979 winner Rubstic and Royal Mail for company, but the latter's blunder at the second-last seemed to gift the race to Aldaniti.

Champion popped him over the last and set off towards the line, but behind him the mighty hunter-chaser Spartan Missile – the 8-1 favourite and twice a winner of the Fox Hunters' Chase – and his partner, 54-year-old John Thorne, were making up ground at the double. With a furlong to run they were close enough to strike fear into Aldaniti's supporters, but Champion was not to be denied at the last and he kept Aldaniti going for a four-length win.

The welcome in the unsaddling enclosure washed over them in a wave of happy tears; those who thought the tale worthy of the Hollywood treatment were 'rewarded' later with the film *Champions*.

Next year Champion and Aldaniti took part in the National again; they fell at the first. Miracles, you see, happen only once.

Steve Dennis

Aldaniti leads Royal Mail over the final fence, with Spartan Missile (striped sleeves) still to deliver a challenge

17
The Aldaniti fairytale

GRAND NATIONAL, AINTREE, APRIL 4, 1981

1. Aldaniti 10-1
2. Spartan Missile 8-1f
3. Royal Mail 16-1

Winning Owner: Nick Embiricos
Trainer: Josh Gifford
Jockey: Bob Champion
Distance: 4l, 2l

Empics

Viking Flagship's quality was beyond question.

He had long been renowned as one of the toughest cookies in the jar, and in Adrian Maguire had the perfect partner with which to complement his brilliance and resilience. The 1995 Mumm Melling Chase was the race that illustrated to best effect the pair's sheer bloody-minded refusal to knuckle under; it was a masterclass in courage.

Viking Flagship was fresh from his second victory in the Queen Mother Champion Chase, fresh from a five-length crushing of Deep Sensation in the hands of Charlie Swan, who had come in for the ride because Maguire had missed the Festival following the death of his mother. He was indisputably the best around at two miles, but had never won over the two and a half of the Melling. The star-crossed Maguire, who would miss the next two Cheltenham Festivals through injury and never win the jockeys' championship that his talents merited, was back in the saddle at Aintree.

Among their five rivals was the oft-maligned Deep Sensation, whose courage at the sticking point had been called into question on more than one occasion in the past, and the Champion Chase third Nakir. A far greater danger, however, was Martha's Son, a specialist at the trip unbeaten in his last nine races – all his chase starts – including a seven-length defeat of Coulton in the Comet Chase at Ascot on his most recent outing.

It must have been the question mark over Viking Flagship's stamina – in comparison with that of Martha's Son – that led punters to send the latter off as hot favourite, but Viking Flagship was never a horse to underestimate and there was still plenty of confidence behind the second favourite.

The trio jumped the last as if glued together and settled down to duke it out

The outsider Southolt set the pace but all the weapons remained safely sheathed until four out, whereupon the 'big three' began to work through the gears. Southolt, still in front at the second-last, was soon swallowed up as Martha's Son hit the front in search of his tenth straight success.

Almost immediately, Deep Sensation, switched to the inside, threw down his challenge. Viking Flagship had been under pressure from three out as Deep Sensation and Martha's Son continued to cruise, but Maguire was now getting a rhythm from his old warhorse and the trio jumped the last as if glued together and settled down to duke it out on the run-in.

To widespread surprise Martha's Son was first to crack but Deep Sensation was a harder nut this time, and it wasn't until the final stride that Maguire, minus his red silk cap, lifted his oh-so-willing partner past Deep Sensation to win by a short head.

Everything had happened so quickly that the three main combatants were not the only ones getting their breath back. The unbeaten record of Martha's Son had gone and Deep Sensation had run the race of his life yet still not won.

However, Viking Flagship's reputation as the doughtiest fighter around was still intact, as was Maguire's as the jockey for whom no cause was lost. The two were made for each other, and never was it better demonstrated.

Steve Dennis

Gerry and Mark Cranham

18
Viking Flagship invincible

MELLING CHASE, AINTREE, APRIL 7, 1995

1. Viking Flagship 5-2
2. Deep Sensation 5-1
3. Martha's Son 11-10f

Winning Owner: Roach Foods Ltd
Trainer: David Nicholson
Jockey: Adrian Maguire
Distance: sh hd, 1l

Martha's Son (left),
Viking Flagship (centre)
and Deep Sensation land
as one over the final
fence

This was the moment: the magic moment. There

had been so many others, that season and in seasons before. Yet, not least because of what would later befall him at Ascot, this was the moment we would cherish most. This was Persian Punch's finest hour.

A problem shared is a problem halved; a pleasure shared is a pleasure doubled. And how we shared that moment. It is rare for an entire racecourse, an entire sport, to come together and will on one horse, regardless of financial interest. When it happens, it is a joyous, uplifting experience. It happened with the Brigadier, it happened with Red Rum and it happened every time Desert Orchid set foot on a racecourse. Likewise, that day at Newmarket, Persian Punch.

How fitting, too, that this was the curtain raiser to Champions Day. For, in winning the 2003 Jockey Club Cup, Persian Punch produced the performance of a champion, if not in strict handicapping terms, then by measures that counted for more than bare numbers. Here, as often before, he embodied courage, heroism and an unquenchable will to win – truly the qualities of a champion. Only 13 days earlier he had been beaten close to 50 lengths in France's premier long-distance race, his ten-year-old legs sinking in a Parisian swamp. That he was competing again so soon was, in itself, something of a surprise. To win at Newmarket was more than could reasonably have been hoped for, not only because of his Longchamp failure, but also because it seemed greedy to expect another triumph at the end of a season

For Persian Punch to win was more than could reasonably have been hoped for

when he had already sparkled with momentous victories at Sandown, Goodwood and Doncaster. One more for the road would surely send his supporters over the limit.

He won the way he liked to win best. Out clear through the early stages, he bowled along merrily, the lead long, the tempo demanding. He stayed in front until two furlongs from home when a half-mile of distress signals culminated in not one, or two, but three of his five rivals ranging alongside before waving goodbye. But then, as his most fearsome opponent, Millenary, began to create clear water, the whip of Richard Hills aboard Tholjanah struck Persian Punch across the nose. The reaction was immediate. Persian Punch did not flinch. Persian Punch fought.

Still fourth entering the final furlong, the old boy summoned up extra reserves, eating the painful final hill, reeling in his adversaries until only one adversary was left. All the time, that adversary, Millenary, was being caught, the crowd all the time close to exploding. As one, they willed him on and he responded, giving all that he had. By the narrowest possible margin, all that he had was enough.

"This place has erupted," remarked Channel 4 commentator Simon Holt, and it had. First paraded back in front of the stands by a jubilant Martin Dwyer, Persian Punch then returned, accompanied by fanfare, to the winner's enclosure, three cheers demanded, three cheers given. At Ascot, six months later, he died. That special day at Newmarket, he was never more alive.

Lee Mottershead

Persian Punch fights his way back into the lead past Millenary in the last strides

19
Persian Punch's finest hour

JOCKEY CLUB CUP, NEWMARKET, OCTOBER 18, 2003

1. Persian Punch 5-2
2. Millenary 15-8f
3. Kasthari 7-2

Winning Owner: Jeff Smith
Trainer: David Elsworth
Jockey: Martin Dwyer
Distance: sh hd, 1l

Gerry and Mark Cranham

It may not have been the greatest race, but

it was surely one of the most exciting, most breathless and most pulsating. At the heart of horseracing is the race itself, and at the heart of the race is the finish, and there can seldom have ever been a better finish than the one that concluded the 2000 Queen Mother Champion Chase.

Replace the horses, the venue and the race, and this would still have been special. Yet thanks to Edredon Bleu and Direct Route, Cheltenham racecourse and the finest two-mile chase in the calendar, this was positively priceless.

Of all the great jump prizes, the Champion Chase is the one that demands perfection. It is the race in which errors are punished more than any other. Racing over the minimum trip at maximum speed, the fastest chasers in town throw themselves over the most demanding track in the country. One blunder, one wrong move, and it can be curtains. It is what multiple champion jockey Tony McCoy calls "the professionals' race". Speaking after the 2000 renewal, he remarked that "of all the races in the world, this was the one I wanted to win most of all". Not only did he win it, but he played a huge part in the most gripping of contests at a wondrous venue renowned for them.

Twelve months earlier, Edredon Bleu had gone close but not close enough, chasing home Call Equiname after that rival had eventually reeled in the habitual front-runner. For his return, Edredon Bleu's task seemed just as hard if not harder, as

It was surely one of the most exciting, most breathless and most pulsating

although Call Equiname was absent, his place was being taken by a Paul Nicholls-trained stablemate, Flagship Uberalles, the previous season's top novice and now the deserved 11-10 favourite. Add in the 1999 third, Direct Route, and you had a powerful triumvirate of top two-mile chasers.

They did not let us down. Charging down the hill to the grandstands and the third-last fence, the big three were the first three. The realisation was matching the anticipation, but for Flagship Uberalles, mistakes at the two obstacles approaching the straight as good as meant game over. Soon after the final fence, his chance was gone. Not so Edredon Bleu and Direct Route. Together they duelled, nigh on inseparable, Edredon Bleu the stands' side, Direct Route the far side, both McCoy and Norman Williamson asking everything of their supremely willing mounts. For a few strides, Williamson had Direct Route's steaming nostrils in front, but for the stride that mattered most, it was McCoy and Edredon Bleu who were ahead. Only just, but only just was enough. They had triumphed in a thriller.

For trainer Henrietta Knight, who had characteristically been unable to watch the race live, it was a moment to rejoice, as it was for McCoy and all blessed to have been present. For the remarkable Edredon Bleu, there would be other remarkable wins, not least in the 2003 King George. Nothing else he did, though, could compare to his Champion Chase.

Lee Mottershead

Gerry and Mark Cranham

20
Edredon Bleu v Direct Route

QUEEN MOTHER CHAMPION CHASE, CHELTENHAM, MARCH 15, 2000

1. Edredon Bleu 7-2
2. Direct Route 5-1
3. Flagship Uberalles 11-10f

Winning Owner: Jim Lewis
Trainer: Henrietta Knight
Jockey: Tony McCoy
Distance: sh hd, 6l

Edredon Bleu (stripes) gets away from the last just ahead of Direct Route, with Flagship Uberalles (stars on cap) beginning to fade

Loose horses and those still with their riders mill around in the melee at the 23rd fence – Foinavon is not pictured; he was long gone

21

Foinavon's fluke

Grand National, Aintree, April 8, 1967

1. **Foinavon** 100-1
2. **Honey End** 15-2f
3. **Red Alligator** 30-1

Winning owner Cyril Watkins **Trainer** John Kempton **Jockey** John Buckingham **Distances** 15l, 3l

What made it great It is highly unlikely that any horserace in history can ever have demonstrated the sport's utter unpredictability more than Foinavon's National. "In a race noted for shocks he can safely be ignored," said that morning's *Daily Express*; his trainer thought so little of his horse's chance that he went to Worcester (where he rode a winner). Yet Foinavon won, simply by virtue of being so slow that he was totally detached from the carnage that took place at the 23rd fence, the one after Becher's on the second circuit. With loose horses and jockeys all over the place, Foinavon picked his plodding way through them all, and by the time any of his rivals got going again, he was too far in front to be caught. **GE**

Empics

Craganour (left) fights off the challenge of Aboyeur – but the stewards had the final word

22

Sensation and tragedy at the Derby

Epsom, June 4, 1913

1. **Aboyeur** 100-1
2. **Louvois** 10-1
3. **Great Sport** 20-1
Disq **Craganour** 6-4f

Winning owner Percy Cunliffe **Trainer** Tom Lewis **Jockey** Edwin Piper **Original distances** hd, nk

What made it great For drama, sensation, tragedy, controversy and intrigue, the 1913 Derby is in a class of its own. A suffragette, Emily Davison, incurred fatal injuries when bringing down the King's horse, Anmer, at Tattenham Corner; and the hot favourite, Craganour, beat long-time leader, 100-1 shot Aboyeur, by a head, only to be disqualified for causing interference. The two principals had battled for the lead all the way up the straight and had looked equally guilty in a very rough race, but the presiding steward, Eustace Loder, who had bred Craganour, had a grudge against the colt's owner, Bower Ismay. The first four had flashed past the post in a uniquely close finish to the premier Classic, and the judge completely missed the third finisher, Day Comet. **JR**

23

Ard Patrick v Sceptre v Rock Sand

Eclipse Stakes, Sandown, July 17, 1903

1. **Ard Patrick** 5-1
2. **Sceptre** 7-4
3. **Rock Sand** 5-4f

Winning owner John Gubbins **Trainer** Sam Darling **Jockey** Otto Madden **Distances** nk, 3l

What made it great The 1903 Eclipse was one of those rare races that are talked about for generations afterwards. Of the three principals, the legendary filly Sceptre had won four of the five Classics the previous season and Rock Sand went on to land that year's Triple Crown, but it was Ard Patrick, the unsung 1902 Derby hero, who emerged victorious. He led on the home turn and, having beaten off Rock Sand halfway up the straight, became locked in a titanic duel with Sceptre. Both four-year-olds responded gamely to pressure and the filly, who was at a disadvantage in terms of fitness and jockeyship, took a slight lead, but Ard Patrick forced his neck in front again on the line. **JR**

Ard Patrick (left) rallies to get the better of the legendary filly Sceptre close home

Press Association / Empics

Michael Dickinson and his five stars (from left) Ashley House, Silver Buck, Wayward Lad, Captain John and Bregawn

24

Dickinson's famous five

Cheltenham Gold Cup, March 17, 1983

1. **Bregawn** 100-30f
2. **Captain John** 11-1
3. **Wayward Lad** 6-1
4. **Silver Buck** 5-1
5. **Ashley House** 12-1

Winning owner Jim Kennelly **Trainer** Michael Dickinson **Jockey** Graham Bradley **Distances** 5l, 1½l

What made it great Never can so much excitement in a championship race have been devoted to the fifth horse home. Ashley House came plodding along a country mile behind his stablemate Bregawn to find himself invited into the most crowded winner's enclosure ever. Bregawn, runner-up the year before, landed the spoils after a fine front-running display, fending off the persistent Captain John over the last two fences and staying on strongly up the hill. Then came Wayward Lad, then Silver Buck. And then everyone was looking for Ashley House. Michael Dickinson had saddled five horses; they were the first five home. "Come on my lot!" he had shouted at the top of the hill. On they came for an unparalleled – and almost unrepeatable – training performance. **SD**

Gerry Cranham

Shergar first, the rest (almost) nowhere

25

Shergar's Derby

Derby, Epsom, June 3, 1981

1. **Shergar** 10-11f
2. **Glint Of Gold** 13-1
3. **Scintillating Air** 50-1

Winning owner Aga Khan IV **Trainer** Michael Stoute
Jockey Walter Swinburn **Distances** 10l, 2l

What made it great An outstanding but ill-fated
champion registered a stunning display when
setting the record for the biggest winning margin in
the history of the Derby. The race looked a foregone
conclusion for Shergar on form and so it proved, for
he was cantering just behind the leaders at
Tattenham Corner and his distinctive rapid, scuttling
stride carried him to an awesome ten-length
triumph. The margin would have been 12 or 15
lengths had he not been eased in the final furlong
by his teenage jockey. Shergar's only two top-class
rivals, Glint Of Gold and Kalaglow, had collided and
virtually put themselves out of the race early on, but
even so his performance was without equal at
Epsom in more than two centuries. **JR**

26

Dubai Millennium's World Cup

Dubai World Cup, Nad Al Sheba, March 25, 2000

1. **Dubai Millennium**
2. **Behrens**
3. **Public Purse**

Winning owner Godolphin **Trainer** Saeed Bin Suroor
Jockey Frankie Dettori **Distances** 6l, 5½l

What made it great Before Dubai Millennium ever set
foot on a racecourse, Sheikh Mohammed changed his
name from Yaazer, believing the colt capable of winning
the millennium edition of the Dubai World Cup. Going
into the race that had long been his destiny, Dubai
Millennium was already being hailed by the Sheikh as the
finest horse Godolphin had owned. In the race Dubai
Millennium was magnificent, setting a gallop so fierce
that most of his rivals were off the bridle at halfway.
Quickening off his own punishing pace, the horse
described as "the best I have seen or had" by his adoring
owner left an indelible memory – a memory made all the
more poignant by his premature death. **LM**

Dubai Millennium has the world at his feet in a night-time annihilation

Edward Whitaker

27

Oh So Sharp by two short heads

1,000 Guineas, Newmarket, May 2, 1985

1. **Oh So Sharp** 2-1f
2. **Al Bahathri** 11-1
3. **Bella Colora** 6-1

Winning owner Sheikh Mohammed **Trainer** Henry Cecil **Jockey** Steve Cauthen **Distances** sh hd, sh hd

What made it great The only British Classic ever to be decided by two short heads, this show-stopping contest was the first jewel in Oh So Sharp's fillies' Triple Crown – and the hardest-earned. Bella Colora, runner-up to Oh So Sharp in the Nell Gwyn Stakes, was sent on after barely a furlong and a half and bowled along in front until Al Bahathri took over approaching the final furlong. At this stage Steve Cauthen was asking the favourite some searching questions and the response was by no means immediate. Bella Colora soon regained the lead from Al Bahathri, but that filly wrested it back in the final strides and looked safely home until Oh So Sharp appeared on the outside to trump all the aces at the death. **SD**

Oh So Sharp swoops late to pip Al Bahathri (centre) and Bella Colora (spots) in the closest finish to a British Classic ever

Gerry and Mark Cranham

APRH

Mandarin (no.1) is in third place as the field takes the water; Fred Winter can be seen struggling with the broken bridlework

28

The miracle of Mandarin

Grand Steeple-Chase de Paris, Auteuil, June 17, 1962

1. **Mandarin** 2-1f
2. **Lumino** 10-1
3. **Paradou** 5-2

Winning owner Peggy Hennessy **Trainer** Fulke Walwyn **Jockey** Fred Winter **Distances** hd, 2½l

What made it great On a hot summer day in Paris, Mandarin and Fred Winter achieved legendary status in France's championship race for steeplechasers. The recent Cheltenham Gold Cup hero, having his last race at the age of 11, had neither steering nor brakes for most of the extended four-mile contest because his bit broke in two approaching the fourth fence. Winter had to rely on the grip of his legs, the distribution of his weight, and his mount's response to the reins on his neck in order to negotiate the Auteuil maze. Always prominent, Mandarin broke down in the closing stages and needed all his courage – and the immense strength of the greatest of all jump jockeys – to hold on in a photo-finish. **JR**

David Leeds / Allsport

29

Tiznow v Sakhee

Breeders' Cup Classic, Belmont Park, October 27, 2001

1. **Tiznow** 69-10
2. **Sakhee** 48-10
3. **Albert The Great** 13-1

Winning owners Michael Cooper & Straub-Rubens Revocable Trust **Trainer** Jay Robbins **Jockey** Chris McCarron **Distances** nose, 1¾l

What made it great On an extraordinary night in New York, Europe had taken the three previous races when Sakhee, record-equalling Arc victor three weeks before, faced dirt for the first time in the Classic. He looked set for a famous victory when Frankie Dettori took him to the front approaching the furlong pole, but that was to reckon without reigning Horse of the Year Tiznow, who had inched out Giant's Causeway in the race 12 months before. The brave US colt became the first horse to win the Classic twice with a near-identical performance, wearing down Sakhee in the dying strides. In the end-of-year rankings Sakhee was officially rated the best horse in the world on his Arc form, 5lb in front of Tiznow. **NG**

Tiznow (centre) gets the better of Sakhee (left) and Albert The Great after a final-furlong duel

Gerry and Mark Cranham

30

El Gran Senor's 2,000 Guineas

2000 Guineas, Newmarket, May 5, 1984

1. **El Gran Senor** 15-8f
2. **Chief Singer** 20-1
3. **Lear Fan** 7-2

Winning owner Robert Sangster **Trainer** Vincent O'Brien **Jockey** Pat Eddery **Distances** 2½l, 4l

What made it great A majestic performance from El Gran Senor, who looked outstanding in destroying a top-class Classic field and maintaining his unbeaten record. Champion two-year-old the previous season, the Ballydoyle colt produced a telling burst of pace just over a furlong out to sweep past the front-running Lear Fan and draw well clear of his rivals, led home by Chief Singer (later a triple Group 1 winner) a respectful distance adrift with the remainder completely strung out behind. Seldom does a racehorse demonstrate an ability to quicken clear of top-class rivals like El Gran Senor did that day. It was one of the greatest Guineas displays ever seen, and showed that he was perhaps the best miler since Brigadier Gerard. **NG**

El Gran Senor's remarkable burst of speed takes him clear of the gallant Chief Singer

31

Tiznow v Giant's Causeway

Breeders' Cup Classic, Churchill Downs, November 4, 2000

1. **Tiznow** 92-10
2. **Giant's Causeway** 76-10
3. **Captain Steve** 136-10

Winning owners Michael Cooper & Cecelia Straub-Rubens **Trainer** Jay Robbins **Jockey** Chris McCarron **Distances** nk, ¾l

What made it great This was a race lost as much as a race won. Tackling dirt for the first time in the last race of his career, Giant's Causeway – dubbed 'the Iron Horse' because of his durability and guts – produced the finest performance of his life, but was still beaten. In an enthralling duel to the line, the Irish star and Tiznow had the race to themselves, the pair pulling clear but the American colt, in his Horse of the Year-clinching performance, refusing to relinquish his narrow advantage. Then, just as Giant's Causeway appeared set to draw level, Mick Kinane got his whip caught in the reins and his mount eased off. For the Iron Horse's supporters, it was a case of what might have been. **LM**

Tiznow (right) gets the better of the 'Iron Horse' Giant's Causeway to land his first Breeders' Cup Classic

Bill Selwyn

Mirror Syndication

Two strides after the line and Lester Piggott and The Minstrel are clear winners – it had been a lot closer a split-second earlier

32

The Minstrel v Hot Grove

Derby, Epsom, June 1, 1977

1. **The Minstrel** 5-1
2. **Hot Grove** 15-1
3. **Blushing Groom** 9-4f

Winning owner Robert Sangster **Trainer** Vincent O'Brien **Jockey** Lester Piggott **Distances** nk, 5l

What made it great With his chestnut coat, big white blaze and four white socks, The Minstrel was always likely to have plenty of knockers. They rocketed out of the woodwork after he was beaten in two Guineas, but if ever a horse had the last laugh, The Minstrel did. He was not the best of Derby winners – indeed, he was not the best three-year-old colt at Ballydoyle that season (Alleged was) – but when it came to courage he could not be faulted, as his Epsom triumph showed. He was under strong pressure to catch Hot Grove well before the final furlong but, responding like a hero to his jockey's powerful pressure, put his head in front in the last couple of strides. He just would not be denied. **GE**

John Crofts

Secreto (left) collars the hitherto unbeaten El Gran Senor in the dying strides to spring a huge shock at Epsom

33

Secreto mugs El Gran Senor

Derby, Epsom, June 6, 1984

1. **Secreto** 14-1
2. **El Gran Senor** 8-11f
3. **Mighty Flutter** 66-1

Winning owner Luigi Miglietti **Trainer** David O'Brien **Jockey** Christy Roche **Distances** sh hd, 3l

What made it great One of the most thrilling and controversial finishes in Derby history, and a major turn-up as the unbeaten El Gran Senor, an outstanding champion at a mile, was upstaged by the unheralded Secreto – and training legend Vincent O'Brien was beaten by his son David. El Gran Senor, sent off odds-on favourite after his brilliant Guineas win, looked set for an emphatic victory when taking the lead two out, still on the bridle. Yet, with the rest of the field beaten, the game, tenacious Secreto stayed on more strongly, finally overcoming his exalted rival right on the line. The drama continued even after the race: Pat Eddery was criticised for not employing the runner-up's blistering acceleration to greater effect, while the rider launched an unavailing objection for alleged leaning. **NG**

34

Marling v Selkirk

Sussex Stakes, Goodwood, July 29, 1992

1. **Marling** 11-10f
2. **Selkirk** 7-2
3. **Second Set** 7-2

Winning owner Edmund Loder **Trainer** Geoff Wragg **Jockey** Pat Eddery
Distances hd, ¾l

What made it great One of the most memorable mile races of the modern era, featuring two top-class exponents of the art in an exhilarating two-furlong duel. After a lung-bursting gallop set by two pacemaking outsiders, the triple Group 1-winning champion filly Marling, who would probably have still been unbeaten but for a luckless passage in that season's Guineas, just held off the champion older horse, four-year-old Selkirk. Nip and tuck all the way as first one, then the other, nosed in front, Marling, under a fierce drive, clawed her way back to score on the nod. Timeform described it as "possibly the most stirring finish of the British season". Take out the "possibly", and you're there. **NG**

The white-faced Selkirk and Marling (rail) fight it out through the final furlong before the filly prevails

Gerry and Mark Cranham

Gerry and Mark Cranham

35

The revenge of Sea Pigeon

Champion Hurdle, Cheltenham, March 11, 1980

1. **Sea Pigeon** 13-2
2. **Monksfield** 6-5f
3. **Birds Nest** 11-1

Winning owner Pat Muldoon **Trainer** Peter Easterby **Jockey** Jonjo O'Neill **Distances** 7l, 1½l

What made it great Yet another unforgettable Champion featuring a pair of horses who were by now national icons. That courageous Irish battler Monksfield had beaten the immensely popular Sea Pigeon, famous for his dramatic burst of acceleration, into second place in the two previous runnings, but now it was time for the latter to claim a hugely cherished, thoroughly deserved and utterly convincing victory. Though there was little between the pair at the final flight, Jonjo O'Neill did not have to get serious to put daylight between Sea Pigeon and his former nemesis, who just held off another old favourite Birds Nest, running in the fifth of his six Champions. A year later, with Monksfield retired, Sea Pigeon was able to achieve parity with him and Night Nurse when landing his second success, thereby confirming his place in the 'holy trinity' of hurdlers. **NG**

Sea Pigeon (centre) follows Monksfield over the last before drawing clear on the run-in; Birds Nest (left) was a game third

36

Best Mate's third Gold Cup

Cheltenham, March 18, 2004

1. **Best Mate** 8-11f
2. **Sir Rembrandt** 33-1
3. **Harbour Pilot** 20-1

Winning owner Jim Lewis **Trainer** Henrietta Knight
Jockey Jim Culloty **Distances** ½l, 1¼l

What made it great Not since Desert Orchid won
the Gold Cup 15 years earlier had Cheltenham
known scenes like those that greeted Best Mate,
after the most beautiful of horses emulated the
incomparable Arkle by winning a third consecutive
Gold Cup. Tension filled the air as the field set off,
but Best Mate's supporters were able to watch
contentedly until the horse, with history at his
hooves, was badly hampered by Harbour Pilot on
the home bend. Then, though, Best Mate engaged
overdrive, powering magnificently into the lead only
to tire up the hill as Sir Rembrandt inched closer. He
held on, though, producing one of racing's defining
moments. **LM**

**Jim Culloty punches
the air as he returns
to unsaddle on Best
Mate; owner Jim
Lewis (front left)
wears an equally
large smile**

Empics

37

Montjeu's King George

**King George II and Queen Elizabeth Diamond Stakes,
Ascot, July 29, 2000**

1. Montjeu 1-3f
2. Fantastic Light 12-1
3. Daliapour 13-2

Winning owner Michael Tabor **Trainer** John Hammond **Jockey**
Mick Kinane **Distances** 1¾l, 3½l

What made it great It had to be seen to be believed. Only six
horses dared take on France's outstanding champion, and such was
Montjeu's reputation that he was sent off a long odds-on favourite.
Dominant in the betting, he was even more dominant in the race.
Never once coming off the bridle, Montjeu cruised into a clear lead
over a furlong out and remained hard held all the way to the line.
Never had Britain's premier weight-for-age race been won with such
contemptuous ease. Described by Mick Kinane as not once out of
"three-parts speed", the regal four-year-old unleashed a
breathtaking performance to record one of the easiest victories seen
in a top-flight contest in recent years. **LM**

**Montjeu barely comes off the
bridle in landing Britain's
biggest midsummer prize**

John Beasley

38

Desert Orchid v Panto Prince

Victor Chandler Chase, Ascot, January 14, 1989

1. **Desert Orchid** 6-4f
2. **Panto Prince** 3-1
3. **Ida's Delight** 66-1

Winning owner Richard Burridge **Trainer** David Elsworth **Jockey** Simon Sherwood **Distances** hd, 8l

What made it great First you win the King George, then you drop back a mile and win the biggest two-mile handicap of the season, and later you win the Gold Cup. If your name is Desert Orchid, that is. The 1988/89 season was his alone, and this never-say-die defeat of a classy rival in Panto Prince underlined both his versatility and his indomitability. Panto Prince was tough, game and consistent and in receipt of 22lb from the grey horse, and when he regained the lead at the last following Desert Orchid's mistake he looked to have the race in safe keeping, especially considering Ascot's short run-in. But Desert Orchid simply could not, would not allow him to win, and he clawed back the deficit to regain the lead on the line. There was no such thing as a lost cause for Desert Orchid. **SD**

Panto Prince has his head in front at the last fence, but Desert Orchid had his grey nose in front where it mattered

Gerry and Mark Cranham

Mill Reef has plenty in hand as he crowns a brilliant year with success in the Prix de l'Arc de Triomphe

39

Mill Reef's Arc

Prix de l'Arc de Triomphe, Longchamp, October 3, 1971

1. **Mill Reef** 7-10f
2. **Pistol Packer** 17-4
3. **Cambrizzia** 39-1

Winning owner Paul Mellon **Trainer** Ian Balding **Jockey** Geoff Lewis **Distances** 3l, 1½l

What made it great A small colt, Mill Reef was a giant in achievement, and never more so than on this autumn day in Paris, when his scintillating Arc victory confirmed both his greatness and his place in the public's affections. Always close up in a race run in record time, he looked in danger of being boxed in early in the straight, but he burst through a gap and into the lead two furlongs out and finished much too strongly for his rivals, who were headed by champion filly Pistol Packer. Mill Reef had already won the Derby and recorded the best performances ever seen in the Eclipse and the King George, but this was the race that earned him immortal fame. **JR**

Universal Pictorial Press

Gerry and Mark Cranham

Dayjur is almost a blur as he barrels to a very easy victory at York

40

Dayjur's Nunthorpe

Nunthorpe Stakes, York, August 23, 1990

1. **Dayjur** 8-11f
2. **Statoblest** 14-1
3. **Pharoah's Delight** 25-1

Winning owner Sheikh Hamdan Al Maktoum **Trainer** Dick Hern **Jockey** Willie Carson **Distances** 4l, 2l

What made it great It didn't last long, but the memories will never fade. Dayjur proved himself the best sprinter of the last 40 years with a performance on the fast Knavesmire turf that has grown in stature as the calibre of modern sprinters has declined. There were no subtleties to Dayjur: he came out of the stalls like a bullet and maintained that speed all the way to the line. What was different at York was that he seemed to step up a gear in the middle of the race; even his overdrive had an overdrive. The clock was the only thing that could keep up with him as he drew right away from his toiling rivals, taking more than a second off the track record and etching himself into sprinting legend. **SD**

Gerry and Mark Cranham

Galileo has the measure of Fantastic Light in the first of their great clashes in the summer of 2001

41

Galileo v Fantastic Light, #1

King George VI and Queen Elizabeth Diamond Stakes, Ascot, July 28, 2001

1. **Galileo** 1-2f
2. **Fantastic Light** 7-2
3. **Hightori** 22-1

Winning owners Sue Magnier & Michael Tabor **Trainer** Aidan O'Brien **Jockey** Mick Kinane **Distances** 2l, 1l

What made it great In many ways it was the perfect clash: Flat racing's two superpowers represented by two exceptional racehorses. For Ballydoyle, Galileo, the silky-smooth Derby winner at Epsom and The Curragh, and for Godolphin, Fantastic Light, two years older and a Group 1 victor in four different countries. The betting favoured Galileo and on this occasion the market was right. Quickening off a fast pace, Galileo surged ahead early in the straight, only to be followed immediately by Fantastic Light. Entering the final furlong the result could have gone either way but, with Fantastic Light's stamina ebbing away up the hill, Galileo opened up clear water for a famous win – but his victim would soon have his revenge. **LM**

Gordon Richards catches his breath as Tudor Minstrel is led in after spreadeagling the opposition in the 2,000 Guineas

42

Tudor Minstrel's 2,000 Guineas

2000 Guineas, Newmarket, April 30, 1947

1. **Tudor Minstrel** 11-8f
2. **Saravan** 25-1
3. **Sayajirao** 33-1

Winning owner John Arthur Dewar **Trainer** Fred Darling **Jockey** Gordon Richards **Distances** 8l, sh hd

What made it great Tudor Minstrel was a brilliant miler, and those who hailed him as the Horse of the Century after his awesome record-breaking victory in the 2,000 Guineas were not far wrong. The previous year's champion juvenile led all the way on a tight rein and, after disposing of Petition (his only serious rival), had the race won before halfway. He cantered past the post with Gordon Richards patting his neck and tweaking his ears, and his official winning margin of eight lengths (photographs show it was at least ten) is easily the biggest ever seen in the race. Tudor Minstrel proved a non-stayer but his Derby flop could not erase the memory of the greatest of all Guineas victories. **JR**

Getty Images

Central Press Photos

Le Moss (left) pulls out all the stops to deny Ardross, who himself won the next two Ascot Gold Cups

43

Le Moss v Ardross #1

Gold Cup, Ascot, June 19, 1980

1. **Le Moss** 3-1f
2. **Ardross** 6-1
3. **Vincent** 11-2

Winning owner Carlo d'Alessio **Trainer** Henry Cecil **Jockey** Joe Mercer **Distances** ¾l, 6l

What made it great In 1980, Le Moss and Ardross were practically the same horse. They fought out the finish of the three most prestigious staying contests in Britain – the Goodwood Cup and Doncaster Cup are the other two – and the winning margins were three-quarters of a length, a neck and a neck, all in favour of Le Moss. But it was the first of their duels, at Royal Ascot, that stood out. Le Moss, following an interrupted schedule and without a preparatory outing, set out to make all as usual, but when Ardross joined issue just inside the two-furlong marker, the lack of race fitness might have been expected to tell. Far from it; every time Ardross looked the stronger, Le Moss dug deep and found a little more. Staying races have never been so exciting, or of such high quality, since that summer. **SD**

44

Mtoto v Reference Point

Eclipse Stakes, Sandown, July 4, 1987

1. **Mtoto** 6-1
2. **Reference Point** evens f
3. **Triptych** 4-1

Winning owner Sheikh Ahmed Al Maktoum **Trainer** Alec Stewart **Jockey** Michael Roberts **Distances** ³/₄l, 1¹/₂l

What made it great A brutal clash of the generations that saw the emergence of a major star in Mtoto. Front-running Reference Point, a thoroughly convincing Derby victor on his previous outing, was sent off hot favourite to add to his laurels over a two-furlong-shorter trip. But for the presence of the year-older Mtoto, a late-maturing colt who became champion older horse twice, he would have done so. Reference Point set a fiercely searching gallop but Mtoto was able to join him two out. However, while a powerful burst of speed became Mtoto's trademark, here that powerful weapon alone was not enough. He could overcome an admirably tenacious rival only after a thrilling struggle in which neither horse was willing to give in. **NG**

Mtoto prevails over Reference Point in a race that marked his arrival in the top echelon

Gerry and Mark Cranham

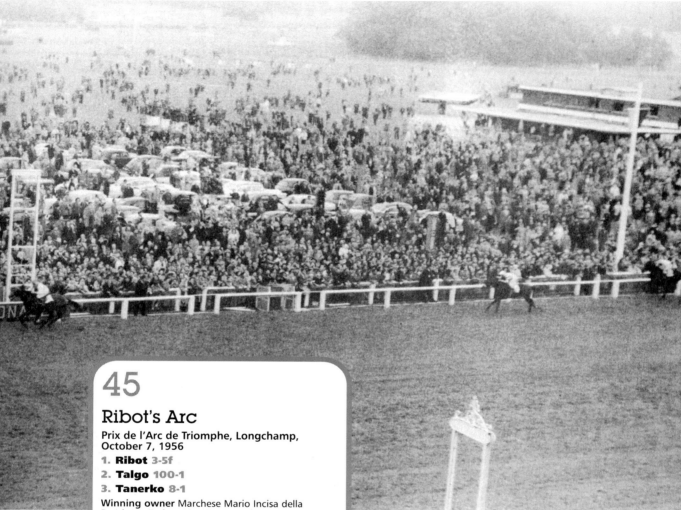

45

Ribot's Arc

Prix de l'Arc de Triomphe, Longchamp, October 7, 1956

1. **Ribot** 3-5f
2. **Talgo** 100-1
3. **Tanerko** 8-1

Winning owner Marchese Mario Incisa della Rocchetta **Trainer** Ugo Penco **Jockey** Enrico Camici **Distances** 6l, 2l

What made it great The legendary Ribot completed his unbeaten 16-race career with a dazzling exhibition of supreme class. The Italian world-beater, bred by Federico Tesio, had already won the Arc once and the King George, and in his second Arc he met a top-quality international field that included two raiders from America. Always in the first three, he took the lead turning for home and, relentlessly striding clear, galloped his rivals into the ground to beat British champion Talgo by an official margin of six lengths, though photographs show the verdict should have been eight or nine lengths. This stunning second victory in Europe's championship race made Ribot a contender for the title Racehorse of the Century. **JR**

Ribot's domination is absolute as Talgo and Tanerko are left trailing

46

The Flying Dutchman v Voltigeur

Match, York, May 13, 1851

1. **The Flying Dutchman** evens
2. **Voltigeur** evens

Winning owner 13th Earl of Eglinton **Trainer** John Fobert **Jockey** Charlie Marlow **Distance** 1l

What made it great The race of the century, and the greatest match race of all time, took place over two miles between two great Yorkshire-trained champions who had both won the Derby and St Leger. In the previous season's Doncaster Cup the year-younger Voltigeur had become the only horse ever to beat The Flying Dutchman, and their second meeting, brought about by popular demand, attracted a huge crowd to the Knavesmire. Voltigeur set the pace and was clear turning for home, but when The Flying Dutchman (conceding the weight-for-age allowance) was asked for an effort it proved irresistible despite a gallant fight by his rival, and he prevailed by a length. **JR**

Thousands watch as The Flying Dutchman gains his revenge on Voltigeur

National Horseracing Museum

Julian Herbert / Allsport

One Man takes the last with a clear lead as he finally ends his Cheltenham Festival drought

47

One Man's Champion Chase

Champion Chase, Cheltenham, March 18, 1998

1. **One Man** 7-2
2. **Or Royal** 7-2
3. **Lord Dorcet** 50-1

Winning owner John Hales **Trainer** Gordon Richards **Jockey** Brian Harding **Distances** 4l, 5l

What made it great One Man was the champion chaser for three consecutive seasons. Like Desert Orchid, he was grey, flamboyant, bold and brilliant but, also like Desert Orchid, Cheltenham was not his ideal track. A beaten favourite in the 1994 Sun Alliance Chase, he had floundered up the hill in the 1996 and 1997 Gold Cups, cruising into a winning position only to walk home exhausted. Yet, dropped back to two miles for the 1998 Champion Chase, One Man replaced pain with pleasure as he made most of the running, stamping his authority on both the field and the hill that had so often hurt him in the past. Tragically, he was killed at Aintree 16 days later. **LM**

48

Royal Palace's Eclipse

The Eclipse, Sandown, July 6, 1968

1. **Royal Palace** 9-4
2. **Taj Dewan** 7-2
3. **Sir Ivor** 4-5f

Winning owner Jim Joel **Trainer** Noel Murless **Jockey** Sandy Barclay **Distances** sh hd, ³/₄l

What made it great Clashes between Derby winners are all too rare, and the meeting of Sir Ivor and the year-older Royal Palace whetted the appetite. Add to that the presence of Taj Dewan, who had been just touched off by Royal Palace in the 2,000 Guineas, and the stage was set for a battle royal. The trio were virtually in a line a furlong from home with Taj Dewan just in front. Sir Ivor, the best horse in the race but below par this time, was the first to admit defeat but Taj Dewan simply refused to let Royal Palace go by. In the last stride Royal Palace forced his nose in front; it took the judge an age to call the result and most thought Taj Dewan had held on. "Merde!" said his trainer when the verdict was given – it does not mean murder. **GE**

Royal Palace pips Taj Dewan (left) by the narrowest of margins, with the below-par Sir Ivor only third

49

Bobsline v Noddy's Ryde

Arkle Challenge Trophy, Cheltenham, March 13, 1984

1. Bobsline 5-4f

2. Noddy's Ryde 7-4

3. Voice Of Progress 6-1

Winning owner Bob Kelsey **Trainer** Francis Flood **Jockey** Frank Berry **Distances** 1½l, 10l

What made it great In the most thrilling novice event in recent memory, the best novice in Ireland went head to head with the best novice in Britain. Expectations were high. They were exceeded. With two to jump Noddy's Ryde was freewheeling in front as usual, with the unbeaten Bobsline on his shoulder, and as the pair turned for home they flattened out like greyhounds and went at it hammer and tongs. They jumped the final fence as one and Bobsline took a slight advantage on the hill before Noddy's Ryde came back at him with an unavailing assault. Bobsline went on to prove himself the senior two-mile champion, but before the year was out Noddy's Ryde was killed in a fall at Devon & Exeter. Everyone felt the loss. **SD**

Bobsline (near side) and Noddy's Ryde take the last as one before fighting out a tremendous battle on the Cheltenham hill

Alec Russell

Bernard Parkin

Flying Wild in the early stages of the Massey-Ferguson, before the race had reached fever pitch

50

Flying Wild floors 'Himself'

Massey-Ferguson Gold Cup, Cheltenham, December 12, 1964

1. **Flying Wild** 100-8
2. **Buona notte** 4-1
3. **Arkle** 8-11f

Winning owner Raymond Guest **Trainer** Dan Moore **Jockey** Tommy Carberry **Distances** sh hd, 1l

What made it great An 'expert' once proclaimed that "handicaps place a premium on mediocrity". If this was mediocrity, let's have it every day, as this was one of the most brilliantly competitive finishes any race has ever produced. Arkle was carrying 12st 10lb, including a 3lb penalty for his win in the Hennessy seven days before; Flying Wild was a top-class mare who had started co-favourite for the previous season's Grand National; and Buona notte had been the previous term's champion novice and was out for the first time that season. Buona notte had been in front when he slipped on landing over the final fence, but he came back so well at Flying Wild that there were only inches between them at the line. Arkle rallied so well up the hill that he was only just behind. Mediocre? Pah! **GE**

51

Dunfermline's jubilee St Leger

St Leger, Doncaster, September 10, 1977

1. **Dunfermline** 10-1
2. **Alleged** 4-7f
3. **Classic Example** 16-1

Winning owner Queen Elizabeth II **Trainer** Dick Hern **Jockey** Willie Carson **Distances** 1½l, 10l

What made it great The Queen's Silver Jubilee year had already been marked in style when her filly Dunfermline won the Oaks, but now the latter was meeting colts including Alleged, who had taken the Great Voltigeur in scintillating style. Take Dunfermline out of the race and Alleged would have won by ten lengths. But she was in it, and when it came to a battle of attrition in the last furlong and a half the Queen's filly was the stronger stayer, and she ground out a notable victory. Lester Piggott probably committed Alleged too soon over a trip beyond his best, but this was still the best single performance by any of the Queen's horses. It was a shame that her duties prevented her witnessing the race in person. **GE**

**Dunfermline (left) gives the Queen her
second Classic in Jubilee year when proving
too strong a stayer for Alleged**

Empics

Mirrorpix

Devon Loch sprawls and sends Dick Francis almost over his ears with 50 yards to run and victory in his grasp – his downfall has never been explained

52

Devon Loch's collapse

Grand National, Aintree, March 24, 1956

1. E.S.B. 100-7
2. Gentle Moya 22-1
3. Royal Tan 28-1

Winning owner Stella Carver **Trainer** Fred Rimell
Jockey Dave Dick **Distances** 10l, 10l

What made it great A victim of cruel luck, Devon
Loch became the most famous loser in racing history
in the saddest and most sensational climax to any
Grand National. The Queen Mother's horse, carrying
11st 4lb, was left in the lead five out and was clear
with the race in safe keeping when he suddenly
sprawled and fell flat on his belly 50 yards from the
line, handing victory to E.S.B. Although the film
suggested Devon Loch had tried to jump an
imaginary fence, his rider, Dick Francis, thinks the
horse was frightened by the deafening cheers of the
crowd. The mystery is still debated. **JR**

Gerry and Mark Cranham

Nothing separates Waterloo Boy (left) and Barnbrook Again at the final fence, and there was only half a length in it at the line in favour of the latter

53

Barnbrook Again – again

Queen Mother Champion Chase, Cheltenham, March 14, 1990

1. **Barnbrook Again** 11-10f
2. **Waterloo Boy** 8-1
3. **Feroda** 9-1

Winning owner Mel Davies **Trainer** David Elsworth **Jockey** Hywel Davies **Distances** ½l, 7l

What made it great No other race at the Cheltenham Festival has produced as many exciting finishes as the Champion Chase, and the 1990 renewal treated racegoers to another cracker. The previous year Barnbrook Again had won this race and Waterloo Boy had taken the Arkle Trophy. Both horses were already established as favourites of the Cheltenham faithful. Locked together up the final hill after shaking off Sabin du Loir, the two principals went head to head, Barnbrook Again hanging all the way to the line but still holding off Waterloo Boy despite the latter's best efforts. Harshly in the eyes of many, both jockeys were banned for excessive use of the whip. **LM**

Martin Lynch

Boreas outruns the eternally gallant Persian Punch to claim the Doncaster Cup

54

Boreas beats Persian Punch

Doncaster Cup, Doncaster, September 12, 2002

1. Boreas 7-2
2. Persian Punch 15-2
3. Darasim 10-1

Winning owner Aston House Stud **Trainer** Luca Cumani **Jockey** Jamie Spencer **Distances** 1¼l, 5l

What made it great Admirable as Boreas was when notching the best victory of his career, the 2002 Doncaster Cup figures in this list because of the runner-up. Persian Punch had been tailed off in the Goodwood Cup, prompting many to call for his retirement, but one week after a minor Salisbury win, he silenced his doubters with a typically gutsy effort on Town Moor. All the way up the straight the nine-year-old stared defeat in the face as Boreas stalked menacingly, but not once did the old boy flinch, plugging on doggedly even when headed by the eventual winner. Boreas was all class, Persian Punch all courage; together they made for a wonderful race. **LM**

55

Stalbridge Colonist and Arkle

Hennessy Gold Cup, Newbury, November 26, 1966

1. **Stalbridge Colonist** 25-1
2. **Arkle** 4-6f
3. **What A Myth** 7-2

Winning owner Ron Blindell **Trainer** Ken Cundell **Jockey** Stan Mellor **Distances** ½l, 1½l

What made it great Such was Arkle's standing that, even though he was making his seasonal reappearance and carrying his inevitable top weight of 12st 7lb, only five were prepared to take him on. He was giving at least 2st to all five and the least likely to beat him was Stalbridge Colonist, who the previous weekend had been beaten more than 40 lengths when last of five finishers at Ascot. Arkle set out to lead all the way and always seemed to be going supremely well in front, but suddenly, going to the last, the possibility of a huge shock developed. Stan Mellor was organising one of his famous 'winding-up' finishes and, halfway up the run-in, the 35lb difference in the weights told for the biggest shock in Hennessy history. Later that season Stalbridge Colonist nearly won the Gold Cup. **GE**

Arkle holds the advantage but Stalbridge Colonist (left) has him in his sights

Press Association / Empics

Getty Images

Persian Punch (far side) shows his legendary battling qualities to see off the sustained challenge of Jardines Lookout

56

Persian Punch v Jardines Lookout

Goodwood Cup, Goodwood, July 31, 2003

1. **Persian Punch** 7-2
2. **Jardines Lookout** 11-2
3. **Savannah Bay** 8-1

Winning owner Jeff Smith **Trainer** David Elsworth **Jockey** Martin Dwyer **Distances** sh hd, 5l

What made it great Seldom before had Goodwood racegoers sprinted from the stands to welcome back a winner, but how they ran after Persian Punch's heroic defeat of Jardines Lookout in one of the finest races ever staged at the course. Having first shaken off Swing Wing, the ten-year-old slugged it out with Jardines Lookout, moving across to eyeball his challenger after being headed early in the straight. Back in front 100 yards from the finish, Persian Punch then had to withstand another attack from his pursuer, grimly hanging on to deafening cheers from the crowd. Wearing dark glasses to hide his tears, David Elsworth remarked that Persian Punch had "even got a crusty old devil like me going a bit soft". **LM**

57

Moscow Flyer v Azertyuiop

Tingle Creek Trophy, Sandown, December 4, 2004

1. **Moscow Flyer** 2-1
2. **Azertyuiop** 5-6f
3. **Well Chief** 6-1

Winning owner Brian Kearney **Trainer** Jessica Harrington **Jockey** Barry Geraghty **Distances** 1½l, sh hd

What made it great Rarely does the realisation match the anticipation, but on this occasion it did. Moscow Flyer and Azertyuiop had clashed twice before, the Irish star coming out on top in the 2003 Tingle Creek before unseating Barry Geraghty in a Champion Chase won in scintillating fashion by his British adversary. When the pair locked horns for the third time, they had already proved themselves among the greatest two-mile steeplechasers ever seen; they lived up to that billing and Well Chief proved that he too fitted that description. Ridden with supreme confidence by Geraghty, who enjoyed a long look over his shoulder approaching the Pond fence, Moscow Flyer was always holding his two rivals up the Sandown hill, triggering rapturous scenes on his return to unsaddle. **LM**

Barry Geraghty salutes the crowd after Moscow Flyer's convincing defeat of Azertyuiop (right) and Well Chief

Edward Whitaker

Press Association

The leaders are not in the picture as Sea Pigeon (right) jumps the second-last ahead of eventual fourth Starfen, but he cut them down with an audacious late thrust

58

Sea Pigeon's second Champion

Champion Hurdle, Cheltenham, March 17, 1981

1. **Sea Pigeon** 7-4f
2. **Pollardstown** 9-1
3. **Daring Run** 8-1

Winning owner Pat Muldoon **Trainer** Peter Easterby **Jockey** John Francome **Distances** 1½l, nk

What made it great Champion Hurdles should not be won with such disdainful arrogance. Fourth in 1977 and second in the next two renewals before finally taking the hurdlers' crown in 1980, Sea Pigeon was 11 years young when returning in 1981. Steered by John Francome in the absence of the injured Jonjo O'Neill, the hugely popular veteran was still three lengths behind Pollardstown when putting in a massive leap at the final flight, and his ice-cool jockey remained motionless until well into the final climb. When the question was eventually popped, hands-and-heels driving was all that was required. "You've never heard such cheers from the crowd," called Peter O'Sullevan as a great champion brought the golden era of hurdling to an end. **LM**

59

Captain Christy's second King George

King George VI Chase, Kempton, December 26, 1975

1. **Captain Christy** 11-10jf
2. **Bula** 11-10jf
3. **Royal Marshal** 33-1

Winning owner Jane Samuel **Trainer** Pat Taaffe **Jockey** Gerry Newman
Distances 30l, 2½l

What made it great Those classic riding instructions of 'jump off in front and keep improving your position' have seldom been better demonstrated than by Captain Christy as he notched his second consecutive victory in Kempton's Christmas showpiece. He could be the most exasperating of horses, as more than once his erratic jumping blundered away golden chances, but when he was good he was brilliant. There was one minor blemish in this round, but it made not the slightest difference as Bula was left struggling in vain pursuit a mile from home. To win the King George by 30 lengths from the best chaser in Britain was the performance of a great champion. **GE**

Captain Christy is out on his own down the back straight with the stands in the distance

Gerry and Mark Cranham

Mirrorpix

Barton Bank leads Bradbury Star away from the last before holding on by a neck after a battle royal

60

Barton Bank v Bradbury Star

King George VI Chase, Kempton, December 27, 1993

1. **Barton Bank** 9-2
2. **Bradbury Star** 5-1
3. **The Fellow** 7-2f

Winning owner Jenny Mould **Trainer** David Nicholson **Jockey** Adrian Maguire **Distances** hd, 10l

What made it great Approaching the penultimate fence of the 1993 King George, five horses were vying for victory. By the time they reached the final fence, five had become two with Barton Bank and Bradbury Star locked in a tingling tussle that had the Christmas crowd roaring its approval. An up-and-coming young name with a tendency to walk through the odd fence, Barton Bank had been ridden aggressively by Adrian Maguire, whereas Mackeson Gold Cup hero Bradbury Star had been nursed into contention by Declan Murphy. On the run to the line they were as one, scrapping for a prize that eventually went the way of Barton Bank. **LM**

Mirrorpix

Montjeu collars El Condor Pasa after looking to be faced with a forlorn task just a furlong earlier

61

Montjeu's Arc

Prix de l'Arc de Triomphe, Longchamp, October 3, 1999

1. **Montjeu** 6-4f
2. **El Condor Pasa** 36-10
3. **Croco Rouge** 14-1

Winning owner Michael Tabor **Trainer** John Hammond **Jockey** Mick Kinane **Distances** ½l, 6l

What made it great Two and a half furlongs from home and the game was up for Montjeu. The Japanese colt El Condor Pasa was five lengths clear and keeping on strongly on the heavy, strength-sapping ground. But then, with a reaction to adversity shown by very few champions, Montjeu rolled up his sleeves and went to work. Kinane pulled him off the rail and into the clear, and the dual Derby hero went in pursuit. El Condor Pasa did not stop, but Montjeu showed wonderful acceleration and determination and collared him 100 yards out. In the end he made it look easy – nothing out of the ordinary for an extraordinary horse. **SD**

62

Swain's first King George

King George VI and Queen Elizabeth Diamond Stakes, Ascot, July 26, 1997

1. **Swain** 16-1
2. **Pilsudski** 6-1
3. **Helissio** 11-10f

Winning owner Godolphin **Trainer** Saeed Bin Suroor **Jockey** John Reid **Distances** 1l, 1¼l

What made it great The advance hype suggested the 1997 King George might turn out to be the greatest race ever. Helissio had won the previous year's Arc by five lengths, Singspiel had victories in the Dubai World Cup and Japan Cup to his name, and the latter's stablemate Pilsudski had netted the Breeders' Cup Turf and Eclipse. Yet the trio were all beaten as Godolphin second string Swain revelled in the soft ground caused by a late downpour to outstay Pilsudski, with Helissio and Singspiel next. The conditions made the result misleading, as it was Pilsudski who was the best horse in Britain in 1997, but he was succeeded by Swain when the latter won his second King George in 1998. **LM**

Swain (left) springs a shock when getting the better of Pilsudski

Mirror Syndication Int. / George Shelton

63

Istabraq the third

Champion Hurdle, Cheltenham, March 14, 2000

1. **Istabraq** 8-15f
2. **Hors La Loi** 11-1
3. **Blue Royal** 16-1

Winning owner John P McManus **Trainer** Aidan O'Brien **Jockey** Charlie Swan **Distances** 4l, nk

What made it great To his legion of Irish fans, Istabraq was already a superstar, but by winning the Champion Hurdle for the third consecutive year the highly strung yet brilliant performer gained immortality. A record-equalling winner of the Champion in 1998 before returning with an easy success 12 months later, Istabraq was not certain to take part in the 2000 renewal until three hours before the race because of a nosebleed the previous night. Against his trainer's better judgement he ran, romping home in record time and in the process becoming the fifth triple winner of the hurdling championship, taking his place alongside Arkle and Golden Miller as one of only three horses to win at four consecutive Cheltenham Festivals. **LM**

Istabraq quickens clear after the last to put distance between himself and his pursuers, led by Blue Royal

Edward Whitaker

Gerry and Mark Cranham

Monksfield (left) and Sea Pigeon in typical Champion Hurdle pose; this time the tough Irishman came out on top

64

Monksfield v Sea Pigeon

Champion Hurdle, Cheltenham, March 14, 1979

1. **Monksfield** 9-4f
2. **Sea Pigeon** 6-1
3. **Beacon Light** 22-1

Winning owner Michael Mangan **Trainer** Des McDonogh **Jockey** Dessie Hughes **Distances** ¾l, 15l

What made it great Put simply, two of the greatest hurdlers ever going at it tooth and claw all the way to the line. This was a vintage Champion – weren't they all in the 1970s? – won by one of the gamest, most resilient and hard-working hurdlers ever in Monksfield, who scored his second consecutive victory in the race over the brilliant Sea Pigeon. The Irish terrier habitually made the running and could be guaranteed to keep it up in the face of whip frenzies from his riders. On this occasion Sea Pigeon made his effort too soon, as Jonjo O'Neill permitted him to edge in front at the final flight and thus allowed Monksfield plenty of time to hit back on the hill, with both horses giving their all. Sea Pigeon gained his revenge 12 months later. **NG**

Press Association / Empics

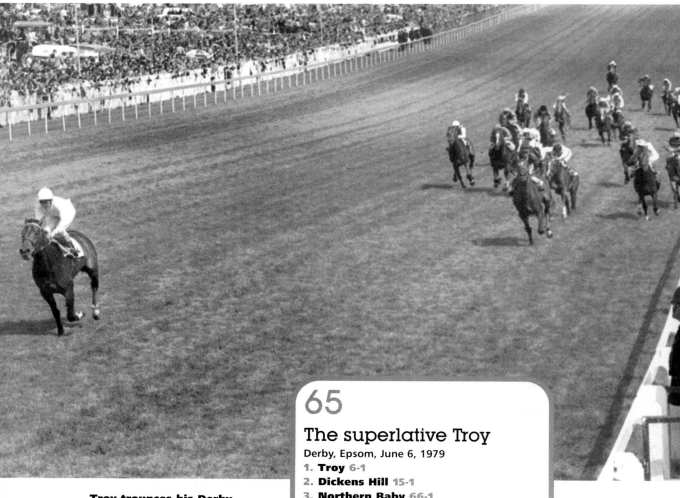

Troy trounces his Derby rivals with a dazzling display of class and speed

65

The superlative Troy

Derby, Epsom, June 6, 1979

1. **Troy** 6-1
2. **Dickens Hill** 15-1
3. **Northern Baby** 66-1

Winning owner Sir Michael Sobell **Trainer** Dick Hern **Jockey** Willie Carson **Distances** 7l, 3l

What made it great Dick Hern had three contenders in the 1979 Derby, the race's 200th running. One of those was the Queen's Milford, who came to Epsom after a wide-margin win in the Lingfield Derby Trial. But for all Milford's claims, you never got the impression that Willie Carson, given the choice as stable jockey, was going to look beyond Troy. He didn't, and he has never regretted it, as Troy spreadeagled his field to win by the biggest margin since Manna triumphed by eight lengths in 1925. It was the performance of a great champion, as he came right away in the final furlong in a manner that simply outclassed his opposition. Such a big day as the 200th Derby deserved a spectacular show, and it certainly got one. **GE**

Phil Cole / Allsport

There's nothing to choose between Travado (left), Deep Sensation (centre) and Viking Flagship at the final fence

66

Viking Flagship's first Champion Chase

Queen Mother Champion Chase, Cheltenham, March 16, 1994

1. **Viking Flagship** 4-1
2. **Travado** 100-30
3. **Deep Sensation** 15-2

Winning owner Roach Foods Ltd **Trainer** David Nicholson **Jockey** Adrian Maguire **Distances** nk, 1l

What made it great The 1994 Queen Mother Champion Chase had everything – a stellar cast featuring the winners of the previous three renewals, mid-race drama, and a pulsating conclusion. On the run to the third-last, the big guns were being kept in reserve until the biggest gun of all, Remittance Man, fell, triggering a huge groan from the stands. The favourite gone, Viking Flagship, Travado and Deep Sensation settled down to fight out a classic finish, the three almost inseparable until the brilliantly brave Viking Flagship edged ahead in the dying strides. One of the toughest chasers of modern times, he returned a year later to successfully defend his title. **LM**

67

Benny The Dip on the nod

Derby, Epsom, June 7, 1997

1. **Benny The Dip** 11-1
2. **Silver Patriarch** 6-1
3. **Romanov** 25-1

Winning owner Landon Knight **Trainer** John Gosden **Jockey** Willie Ryan **Distances** sh hd, 5l

What made it great This was not a 'great' renewal of the Derby, but the principals contrived an unforgettable finish. A lacklustre line-up was led by 2,000 Guineas winner Entrepreneur, sent away at odds-on but destined only for fourth. The race was transformed when Dante winner Benny The Dip and Willie Ryan went for home after rounding Tattenham Corner, the pair stretching six lengths clear with two furlongs to run. The only threat was Silver Patriarch, who reeled in the leader as if he were standing still in the final furlong and put his head in front a stride after the line. *After the line*. Benny The Dip had done just enough; Silver Patriarch had to wait until the St Leger for his Classic win. **SD**

Silver Patriarch (left) comes with a storming late run that fails by the narrowest margin to peg back Benny The Dip

Phil Cole / Allsport

Bill Selwyn

**Hawk Wing wins the
Lockinge, looking for all the
world as comfortable as he
did when going to post**

68

Hail the Hawk

Lockinge Stakes, Newbury, May 17, 2003

1. **Hawk Wing** 2-1f
2. **Where Or When** 7-2
3. **Olden Times** 10-1

Winning owner Sue Magnier **Trainer** Aidan O'Brien **Jockey** Mick Kinane
Distances 11l, 8l

What made it great Aidan O'Brien had always insisted that Hawk Wing
was capable of great things but the horse had never proved it. Second in
the 2,000 Guineas, Derby, Irish Champion Stakes and Queen Elizabeth II
Stakes at three, Hawk Wing had lost much of his lustre by the time he
made his seasonal reappearance in the Lockinge, but what he did at
Newbury was scarcely credible. Making all up the centre of the track, the
impossibly handsome colt ran his rivals ragged, powering clear to win by
an enormous margin and producing a performance that caused ill-
informed comparisons with Brigadier Gerard and El Gran Senor. He still had
plenty of critics and was never able to do it again, being retired after his
next race. **LM**

Mirrorpix

Tony McCoy gets a bold leap out of Pridwell (right) as he comes to challenge Istabraq in the mud at Aintree

69

Tony McCoy and Pridwell

Aintree Hurdle, Aintree, April 4, 1998

1. **Pridwell** 6-1
2. **Istabraq** 4-7f
3. **Kerawi** 10-1

Winning owners Jones, Berstock and Fleet Partnership **Trainer** Martin Pipe **Jockey** Tony McCoy **Distances** hd, 26l

What made it great One man did – his name was Tony McCoy. Awful ground, a muddling pace, a trip in excess of his best and a dangerous rival on a 'going' day all conspired to prise open newly crowned champion hurdler Istabraq's cloak of invincibility after ten consecutive victories. It would have been 11 but for an inspired McCoy, who forced the quirky, often recalcitrant Pridwell, labelled a 'monkey' and worse, to give his all in a power-packed finish. Given the conditions, Pridwell had every excuse to down tools, especially meeting a great rival at level weights, but McCoy simply demanded that he rally all the way to the line to claim the biggest of scalps – plus a controversial whip ban for the jockey! **NG**

Getty Images

Alycidon strolls home to underline his status as the best stayer of the post-war period

70

Alycidon v Black Tarquin

Gold Cup, Ascot, June 16, 1949

1. **Alycidon** 5-4
2. **Black Tarquin** 11-10f
3. **Heron Bridge** 25-1

Winning owner 18th Earl of Derby **Trainer** Walter Earl **Jockey** Doug Smith
Distances 5l, 10l

What made it great In an epoch-making Ascot Gold Cup, Alycidon proved himself the greatest stayer of the post-war era by trouncing reigning champion Black Tarquin, who had beaten him into second place in the previous year's St Leger. After his pacemakers Stockbridge and Benny Lynch had done their job to perfection, the blinkered Alycidon took the lead five furlongs from home, and although Black Tarquin ranged almost upsides him early in the straight, his relentless stride soon told and he galloped the favourite into submission. He went on to become the first winner of the stayers' triple crown in 70 years. **JR**

71

Sea-Bird: the greatest Derby winner

Derby, Epsom, June 2, 1965

1. **Sea-Bird** 7-4f
2. **Meadow Court** 10-1
3. **I Say** 28-1

Winning owner Jean Ternynck **Trainer** Etienne Pollet **Jockey** Pat Glennon **Distances** 2l, 1½l

Why it was great The legendary Sea-Bird won the Derby without coming off the bridle in an awesome display of class. Having started slowly, the French colt cantered to the front over a furlong from home and, briefly pushed out, opened up a four-length lead within 100 yards before being eased; his final margin over subsequent Irish Derby and King George victor Meadow Court gave no indication of his superiority. Even after his dazzling Arc victory, Sea-Bird had rivals for the title 'Flat Horse of the Century', but his status as the supreme Derby winner is beyond dispute. **JR**

Sea-Bird doesn't even break sweat as he comes home with his ears pricked from the top-class Meadow Court

Press Association / Empics

Sir Ivor (left) shows an exceptional turn of foot to cut down Connaught and win easing up

72

Sir Ivor's Derby

Derby, Epsom, May 29, 1968

1. **Sir Ivor** 4-5f
2. **Connaught** 100-9
3. **Mount Athos** 45-1

Winning owner Raymond Guest **Trainer** Vincent O'Brien **Jockey** Lester Piggott **Distances** 1½l, 2½l

What made it great For many months, the bookmaker William Hill and the senior members of his team had been gazing gloomily at one particular line in their ante-post Derby book – the line recording the bet they had laid to US ambassador to Ireland Raymond Guest at 500-1 that his colt Sir Ivor would win the Derby. In the race itself Hill had one big hope, about three furlongs out when Connaught was making boldly for home and Sir Ivor had a formidable amount to do to catch him. Perhaps the task would be beyond him. It wasn't. When Piggott began Sir Ivor's run there was not a moment's doubt, and although Connaught was not stopping, Sir Ivor swept past as if he were standing still. His finishing pace was nothing short of breathtaking. **GE**

Empics

Pendil leads over the last with a clear advantage, but The Dikler (left) stayed on gamely to collar him close home

73

The Dikler and Pendil

Cheltenham Gold Cup, March 15, 1973

1. The Dikler 9-1
2. Pendil 4-6f
3. Charlie Potheen 9-2

Winning owner Peggy August **Trainer** Fulke Walwyn **Jockey** Ron Barry **Distances** sh hd, 6l

What made it great It was a match between the classic steeplechaser, one of the most brilliant jumpers of all time, and the rough-and-ready rival. Pendil was the epitome of what a top-class staying chaser should be – he just did everything right – while The Dikler was one of the most testing of rides, though his enthusiasm for a battle could not be questioned. When Pendil hit the front at the second-last he looked sure to win, and nothing had altered that impression at the last, but in the face of deafening cheers from the crowd he faltered halfway up the hill and The Dikler put his nose in front 75 yards from home. Pendil rallied in the dying strides but, in one of the most misleading of Gold Cup results, The Dikler was still in front when it mattered. **GE**

Edward Whitaker

Iris's Gift (right) delivers the challenge that ultimately prevented Baracouda clinching a Stayers' Hurdle hat-trick

74

Iris's Gift v Baracouda

Stayers' Hurdle, Cheltenham, March 18, 2004

1. **Iris's Gift** 9-2
2. **Baracouda** 8-11f
3. **Crystal d'Ainay** 8-1

Winning owner Robert Lester **Trainer** Jonjo O'Neill **Jockey** Barry Geraghty **Distances** 1½l, 13l

What made it great Relatively recent races, fresh in the mind, are likely to hold an advantage over races of older vintage when it comes to a public vote. That may partly explain how the eclipse of an outstanding horse such as Baracouda, the best winner in the history of the Stayers' Hurdle, figures quite so high, although this was a stirring contest in its own right in which the two principals were both champion hurdlers. Iris's Gift was kicked on with conviction two out in a bid to spike the favourite's guns. Baracouda, who had won the two previous runnings of the race, closed menacingly in trademark fashion at the last, but his steel-grey rival was not to be denied in a rousing battle. **NG**

75

Sea Pigeon's Ebor

Ebor Handicap, York, August 22, 1979

1. Sea Pigeon 18-1
2. Donegal Prince 33-1
3. Move Off 12-1

Winning owner Pat Muldoon **Trainer** Peter Easterby
Jockey Jonjo O'Neill **Distances** sh hd, 2½l

What made it great Mention of Sea Pigeon evokes
memories of the golden era of hurdling and a thrillingly
potent turn of foot, yet this immensely popular horse was
responsible for a handful of memorable days on the Flat as
well – none more so than this typically dramatic victory in
the Ebor Handicap. Despite his glittering dual-purpose CV,
an SP of 18-1 reflected the size of the nine-year-old's task
in shouldering top weight of 10st under regular jumps
partner Jonjo O'Neill. Sea Pigeon swept to the front inside
the final furlong to record an improbable, never-to-be-
forgotten success in front of the locals. Only just, though,
as O'Neill sent the hearts of the Knavesmire crowd into
their mouths when he dropped his hands a couple of
strides from home and nearly threw the race away. **NG**

**Sea Pigeon (left) delights the
Yorkshire crowd when
hanging on by the narrowest
margin from Donegal Prince**

Sporting Pictures

Lanzarote (right) lands first at the last and Comedy Of Errors can't peg him back on the run-in

76

Lanzarote v Comedy Of Errors

Champion Hurdle, Cheltenham, March 13, 1974

1. Lanzarote 7-4

2. Comedy Of Errors 4-6f

3. Yenisei 100-1

Winning owner Lord Howard de Walden **Trainer** Fred Winter **Jockey** Richard Pitman **Distances** 3l, 8l

Why it was great Comedy Of Errors, winner of the Champion Hurdle 12 months before, and Lanzarote dominated the hurdling scene – so much so that only five, one of whom was Lanzarote's 300-1 pacemaker, were prepared to take them on at Cheltenham. The big two had not met during the season, in which Lanzarote was unbeaten in five starts and Comedy Of Errors had won four from five, so Cheltenham was to be the real showdown. Lanzarote threw down the gauntlet at the top of the hill and the lead he stole there proved decisive in what may have been a misleading result. Battle was well and truly joined at the second-last and Comedy Of Errors did his best, but Lanzarote galloped on too strongly. **GE**

77

The Carvill's Hill controversy

Cheltenham Gold Cup, March 12, 1992

1. Cool Ground 25-1
2. The Fellow 7-2
3. Docklands Express 16-1

Winning owner Whitcombe Manor Racing Stables **Trainer** Toby Balding **Jockey** Adrian Maguire **Distances** sh hd, 1l

Why it was great The brilliant but brittle Carvill's Hill took centre stage in one of the most controversial Gold Cups ever. An even-money favourite, he took the first fence by the roots and was then prevented from settling in front by the no-hoper Golden Freeze, who noticeably put him off his stride by continually jumping up alongside him. When the harried favourite cried enough two out a titanic three-horse battle ensued, which looked likely to be won by The Fellow – who had been beaten a short head the previous year – until the hitherto unconsidered Cool Ground was galvanised to steal the prize close home. He would not have won had Adrian Maguire not broken the rule about excessive use of the whip. **SD**

The Fellow (left) has to settle for the runner-up spot again as Adrian Maguire drives Cool Ground past him

Getty Images

Gerry and Mark Cranham

Oh So Sharp (rail) loses her unbeaten record as Petoski comes up the centre of the track to spring a shock

78

Petoski stuns Oh So Sharp

King George, Ascot, July 27, 1985

1. **Petoski** 12-1
2. **Oh So Sharp** 4-5f
3. **Rainbow Quest** 12-1

Winning owner Lady Beaverbrook **Trainer** Dick Hern **Jockey** Willie Carson
Distances nk, ¾l

What made it great Although Oh So Sharp had two Classics – the 1,000 Guineas and Oaks – already to her credit, she was initially her stable's second string for the race and was pressed into the front line only when Derby hero Slip Anchor was unable to run. It is a tribute to her status that she started at odds-on against a distinguished international field, and a tribute to her rivals that they took her on. Petoski, well beaten in the Derby, had won the Princess of Wales's Stakes on his most recent outing and now produced the performance of his life to end the filly's unbeaten record. The pair had a battle royal through the final furlong, with neither giving an inch, and Petoski's determination got him home in a thrilling finish. **GE**

Sportsphoto

See More Business (left) joins battle with Go Ballistic on the hill before grinding out a deserved success

79

See More's Gold Cup

Cheltenham Gold Cup, March 18, 1999

1. See More Business 16-1
2. Go Ballistic 66-1
3. Florida Pearl 5-2f

Winning owners Paul Barber & John Keighley
Trainer Paul Nicholls **Jockey** Mick Fitzgerald
Distances 1l, 17l

What made it great This was not the most competitive Gold Cup in living memory, and its position in this poll is entirely attributable to the identity of the horse who won it, as See More Business was one of the best-loved steeplechasers of recent seasons. Those who kept faith with him after some moderate performances – he even wore blinkers for the first time – received handsome reward as, all out, he knuckled down to hold off outsider Go Ballistic up the hill. It was not his best performance but it was his most important. There was also some poetic justice about it, as he had been carried out during the early stages when much better fancied for the previous year's Gold Cup. **NG**

80

Dubai rules Royal Ascot

Prince of Wales's Stakes, Ascot, June 21, 2000

1. Dubai Millennium 5-4f
2. Sumitas 66-1
3. Beat All 14-1

Winning owner Godolphin **Trainer** Saeed Bin Suroor **Jockey** Jerry Bailey **Distances** 8l, ½l

What made it great After his ruthless performance in the Dubai World Cup on sand, Sheikh Mohammed's best and favourite horse produced another superlative effort back on turf. Although the race was billed as a match between the Godolphin superstar and top French miler Sendawar, the latter paid the price for trying to keep tabs on his front-running rival in the early stages. As Sendawar fell apart, Dubai Millennium powered extravagantly clear of the remainder in the style of a great champion to take his overall record to seven wins from eight starts. Such a display of supreme dominance is seldom seen at Royal Ascot, but it proved to be the colt's last appearance. His career was soon ended by injury and, at the age of five, his life was claimed by grass sickness. **NG**

Dubai Millennium strolls home with imperious ease in what proved to be his last racecourse appearance

Edward Whitaker

81

Hermit's Derby sensation

Derby, Epsom, May 22, 1867

1. **Hermit** 1,000-15
2. **Marksman** 10-1
3. **Vauban** 6-4f

Winning owner Henry Chaplin **Trainer** George Bloss **Jockey** John Daley **Distances** nk, bad

Why it was great The 1867 Derby had a sensational background, partly because the winner's odds lengthened dramatically to 66-1 when he broke a blood vessel a few days before the race. Hermit, though the best colt of his year and later a great sire, looked forlorn on this snowy day at Epsom, but he was not rattled by the many false starts and, producing a strong late run, just caught Marksman, whose rider may have been caught napping. Three years before, his owner's fiancée had eloped with the Marquess of Hastings; the latter bet heavily against Hermit in the Derby and the result hastened his ruin. **JR**

Hermit, the Derby winner who broke the Marquess of Hastings' heart

Getty Images / Time Life Pictures

Edward Whitaker

Giant's Causeway (left) shows his hallmark courage to deny Kalanisi in the dying strides

82

The Iron Horse proves his mettle

Eclipse Stakes, Sandown, July 8, 2000

1. **Giant's Causeway** 8-1
2. **Kalanisi** 7-2
3. **Shiva** 4-1

Winning owners Sue Magnier & Michael Tabor **Trainer** Aidan O'Brien **Jockey** George Duffield **Distances** hd, 2½l

What made it great They called him 'the Iron Horse' and this was the race that forged that sobriquet. Winner of an average St James's Palace Stakes on his previous start, Giant's Causeway took on his elders for the first time at Sandown – Fantastic Light and his contemporary Sakhee were among his rivals – and set his seal on the summer with the grittiest of displays. Duffield sent him on two furlongs out and made the best of his way home, but Pat Eddery had Kalanisi in top gear at the furlong pole and the Aga Khan's colt put his head in front. However, Giant's Causeway took that kind of thing personally and, in a bitter battle, found the reserves to regain the advantage almost on the line. He was to repeat the dose again and again. **SD**

83

Isio v Azertyuiop

Victor Chandler Chase, Ascot, January 10, 2004

1. **Isio** 4-1
2. **Azertyuiop** 7-2f
3. **Got One Too** 33-1

Winning owners Sir Peter & Lady Gibbings **Trainer** Nicky Henderson
Jockey Mick Fitzgerald **Distances** nk, 9l

What made it great If any horse can be said to have had his reputation enhanced by coming off second-best in a duel, it is Azertyuiop. Winner of the Arkle Trophy the previous season, he carried top weight of 11st 10lb in this handicap, and although he loomed up to challenge Isio at the second-last, it looked odds-on that his burden would prove his downfall. Weight can stop trains, but it didn't hold Azertyuiop back and Ruby Walsh drove him into the lead after the last. Isio fought bravely and Azertyuiop countered; it wasn't until the final 50 yards that Isio made his 19lb concession count. Azertyuiop may have lost the race but the honours were his. **SD**

Isio (near side) holds a narrow advantage over Azertyuiop after the last and had to dig deep to hold on to it

Gerry and Mark Cranham

84

Ormonde v Minting

2,000 Guineas, Newmarket, April 28, 1886

1. **Ormonde** 7-2
2. **Minting** 11-10f
3. **Mephisto** 100-3

Winning owner 1st Duke of Westminster **Trainer** John Porter
Jockey George Barrett **Distances** 2l, 10l

Why it was great Unbeaten in a career of 16 races, Ormonde
was the greatest racehorse of the 19th century, and en route to
Triple Crown glory he overcame the brilliant Minting in a
celebrated duel for the 2,000 Guineas. The two principals raced
side by side and their battle for supremacy carried them clear.
Minting, the champion two-year-old whose trainer had refused
to admit the possibility of defeat, briefly forced his head in front
running down the hill, but he then became unbalanced and
Ormonde went clear in the Dip to prove himself the best of an
exceptional crop of three-year-olds. **JR**

**Ormonde, unbeaten in 16 starts
and the greatest racehorse of the
19th century**

Getty Images / Time Life Pictures

85

Pebbles takes the mickey

Champion Stakes, Newmarket, October 19, 1985

1. **Pebbles** 9-2
2. **Slip Anchor** 6-4f
3. **Palace Music** 14-1

Winning owner Sheikh Mohammed **Trainer** Clive Brittain **Jockey** Pat Eddery **Distances** 3l, hd

What made it great Having become the first filly to win the Eclipse, this popular four-year-old returned from a mid-season break to prove herself among the greatest fillies in Turf history with this astonishing performance, in which she comfortably accounted for Derby hero Slip Anchor. Worried about Pebbles' tendency to pull, Pat Eddery dropped her out early on before switching to the rails two furlongs out and easing her past a top-class field. Pebbles won going away, hard held. "I don't think I've ever ridden an easier Group 1 winner," said Eddery years later. The partnership wasn't done yet, either. Next time out they won the Breeders' Cup Turf. **NG**

Pat Eddery looks round for dangers – there are none – as Pebbles scoots clear of a top-class field

Gerry and Mark Cranham

Getty Images

Arkle leads Mill House in the early stages of a victory that was his last and most conclusive over the 'Big Horse'

86

Arkle supreme

Gallaher Gold Cup, Sandown, November 6, 1965

1. **Arkle** 4-9f
2. **Rondetto** 9-1
3. **Mill House** 7-2

Winning owner Anne Duchess of Westminster **Trainer** Tom Dreaper **Jockey** Pat Taaffe **Distances** 20l, 4l

Why it was great Arkle conceded lumps of weight to top-class horses in a handicap, and proved himself beyond doubt the supreme steeplechaser with a dazzling performance. Carrying his usual burden of 12st 7lb, he was meeting former champion Mill House for the fifth and final time, and many thought that his arch-rival, receiving 16lb, had a real chance of success, especially when he jumped superbly in the lead on the second circuit. However, Arkle turned on the power before the Pond fence and cruised home in record time, crushing his opponents with a display of overwhelming class that no other jumper has ever been able to match. **JR**

87

Shahrastani and Dancing Brave

Derby, Epsom, June 4, 1986

1. **Shahrastani** 11-2
2. **Dancing Brave** 2-1f
3. **Mashkour** 12-1

Winning owner Aga Khan IV **Trainer** Michael Stoute **Jockey** Walter Swinburn **Distances** ½l, 2½l

What made it great It was lucky for Greville Starkey that there was not a lynch mob at Epsom on this June afternoon. Nearly all observers were convinced that Dancing Brave should have won the Derby instead of being beaten by a fast-diminishing half-length, and controversy has raged ever since, all the more so as subsequent events showed that he was by far the best horse in the race. Circumstances conspired against Starkey, especially as his mount became unbalanced on the Epsom switchback, and it was testimony to Dancing Brave's brilliance that he got as close as he did after being given too much to do. It was a day of high drama, as befits the world's most famous Classic. **GE**

Dancing Brave's barnstorming finish is not enough to peg back Shahrastani in a race that is still hotly debated

Mirror Syndication

88

Norton's Coin: shock of the century

Cheltenham Gold Cup, March 15, 1990

1. **Norton's Coin** 100-1
2. **Toby Tobias** 8-1
3. **Desert Orchid** 10-11f

Winning owner Sirrell Griffiths **Trainer** Sirrell Griffiths **Jockey** Graham McCourt **Distances** ¾l, 4l

What made it great One of the big advantages that jumping has over Flat racing is that every so often its biggest races fall to the 'little man'. You cannot imagine a man with a runner in the Derby starting his day by milking a herd of cows, but that is what Sirrell Griffiths did before he set out for Cheltenham from his farm at Nantgaredig in south Wales. No-one gave Norton's Coin a prayer – he had been beaten 15 lengths in a handicap on his previous appearance – but for some inexplicable reason he chose this huge day to run vastly better than he had ever done before or, indeed, did afterwards. It was a wonderful example of David taking on and beating Goliath, and the generous Cheltenham crowd took the Carmarthenshire dairy farmer to their hearts. **GE**

Norton's Coin (left) gets the better of Toby Tobias to spring the biggest shock in Gold Cup history

Getty Images

Gerry and Mark Cranham

"I bet he drinks Carling Black Label"

89

Rhyme 'N' Reason: down but not out

Grand National, Aintree, April 9, 1988

1. Rhyme 'N' Reason 10-1

2. Durham Edition 20-1

3. Monanore 33-1

Winning owner Juliet Reed **Trainer** David Elsworth **Jockey** Brendan Powell **Distances** 4l, 15l

What made it great The form-book says "blundered badly 6th". It is a miracle of understatement. What happened was that Rhyme 'N' Reason cleared Becher's first time round, sprawled like a cartoon horse, slid along on his stomach, dragged himself to his feet and set off in pursuit of the field at a walk, last of the 33 still standing. Perseverance seemed futile, yet five from home he was in the lead. On the run to the last he looked held in second behind Durham Edition, but the tenacity that had brought him back into the race proved his ally once again, as he fought back, regained the lead 100 yards out and won going away under his burden of 11st. He had stared defeat in the eye twice but was not to be denied his finest hour. **SD**

Rhyme 'N' Reason (left, light colours) begins to drag himself to his feet after almost falling at Becher's first time

90

Specify: the closest-ever Grand National

Grand National, Aintree, April 3, 1971

1. **Specify** 28-1
2. **Black Secret** 20-1
3. **Astbury** 33-1

Winning owner Fred Pontin **Trainer** John Sutcliffe snr
Jockey John Cook **Distances** nk, 2½l

What made it great Every so often the Grand National produces a close finish between two horses. Sometimes there is one with three protagonists, but to have five horses in with a chance after the final fence made this the closest finish the great race has ever produced. Maybe the mare Sandy Sprite, who led over the last before finishing fifth, might have won if she had not broken down, and then there was the prospect of Jim Dreaper on Black Secret winning the National on his very first ride at Aintree. But, just as he looked as if he was going to win the race that had always eluded his illustrious father Tom, John Cook got a dream run along the rail to snatch the prize in the dying strides. Less than five lengths covered the first five home. **GE**

Specify squeezes through on the rail to thwart Black Secret (spots) by just a neck after four and a half miles

Mirror Syndication

Gerry and Mark Cranham

Slip Anchor stamps his authority by strolling home from Law Society (left) and Damister (white sleeves)

91

Slip Anchor's Derby

Derby, Epsom, June 5, 1985

1. **Slip Anchor** 9-4f
2. **Law Society** 5-1
3. **Damister** 16-1

Winning owner Lord Howard de Walden
Trainer Henry Cecil **Jockey** Steve Cauthen
Distances 7l, 6l

What made it great "He'll gallop them into the ground," was what Cauthen prophesied after Slip Anchor had come home alone in the Derby Trial at Lingfield. Whether he envisaged a display of quite such domination may be another thing, but Slip Anchor led from start to finish at Epsom and can barely have seen another runner. He was in a clear lead from before halfway and all the way up the straight he became more and more imperious as his opponents vainly tried to mount a challenge. Nothing was ever going to materialise and the apricot colours came home on their own. Total superiority by an outstanding champion who, however, never won again. **GE**

92

Dr Devious v St Jovite

Irish Champion Stakes, Leopardstown, September 13, 1992

1. **Dr Devious** 7-2
2. **St Jovite** 4-7f
3. **Alflora** 50-1

Winning owner Sidney Craig **Trainer** Peter Chapple-Hyam **Jockey** John Reid **Distances** sh hd, 9l

What made it great Best of three would settle it. Two high-class middle-distance colts, each with a Derby to his name, turned up at Leopardstown primed to fight to the finish. Dr Devious had beaten St Jovite by two lengths at Epsom; St Jovite had taken that punch and hit Dr Devious for six – actually 12 lengths – at The Curragh before coasting home with the King George in the Doctor's absence. Christy Roche set out to make St Jovite's stamina tell, but Dr Devious joined him at the furlong pole and the pair ran eye to eye to the line, no quarter given, none asked. Dr Devious had a whisker in front when the camera clicked but neither deserved to lose. Though the result went against him, St Jovite's previous exploits had already secured him the status of the best horse in Europe. **SD**

St Jovite (left) and Dr Devious give their all inside the final furlong of a pulsating Irish Champion Stakes

Caroline Norris

Empics

93

Mill House's last hurrah

Whitbread Gold Cup, Sandown, April 29, 1967

1. **Mill House** 9-2f
2. **Kapeno** 100-8
3. **Kellsboro' Wood** 100-7

Winning owner Bill Gollings **Trainer** Fulke Walwyn
Jockey David Nicholson **Distances** 1½l, 1½l

What made it great Having lived for so long in the
shadow of Arkle, Mill House had what many felt would
be his last chance to win a major race. On a brilliantly
sunny afternoon he jumped with all his old élan and,
despite shouldering 11st 11lb, made just about all the
running. He was getting tired after the final fence and
David Nicholson, deputising for the injured Willie
Robinson, must have felt that the post would never
come in the face of Kapeno's strong late dash. But Mill
House lasted home to the unrestrained delight of the
Sandown crowd, who rushed to give the great champion
the hero's reception he deserved. Grown men were seen
to stiffen their lips; it was that kind of race. **GE**

**Mill House bounces back for an
emotional big-race success to
evoke memories of the brilliance
of his younger days**

Illustrated London News

Quashed (near side) denies US Triple Crown winner Omaha in one of the earliest transatlantic clashes

94

Quashed v Omaha

Gold Cup, Ascot, June 18, 1936

1. **Quashed** 3-1
2. **Omaha** 11-8f
3. **Bokbul** 100-6

Winning owner Lord Stanley **Trainer** Colledge Leader **Jockey** Dick Perryman **Distances** sh hd, 5l

What made it great One of the earliest transatlantic clashes pitched an Oaks winner against a US Triple Crown victor, and produced a famous duel from which the filly, Quashed, emerged as the toast of British racing. Having taken the lead early in the Ascot straight, she was joined by the American colt, Omaha, over a furlong from home, and the two four-year-olds battled it out courageously until they passed the post almost inseparable; the judge gave the verdict to the British flag-bearer. Sales director Somerville Tattersall echoed the thoughts of many when he said: "Quashed is the gamest mare of all time." **JR**

95

Frankie's magnificent seven

Gordon Carter Handicap, Ascot, September 28, 1996

1. **Fujiyama Crest** 2-1f
2. **Northern Fleet** 9-1
3. **Miroswaki** 12-1

Winning owner Seisuke Hata **Trainer** Michael Stoute **Jockey** Frankie Dettori **Distances** nk, 2l

What made it great Six down, one to go. Dettori had taken Ascot by storm, evoking comparison with Gordon Richards, who rode all six winners on a Chepstow card in October 1933. Not a soul left the track before the last – the BBC altered its schedule to broadcast the race – in which Dettori set out to make all, and as Fujiyama Crest turned into the straight in front the crowd rose in acclamation and yelled him home. Pat Eddery and Northern Fleet threw down a challenge from the distance but Dettori was, on this day of days, an irresistible force. The crowd round the winner's enclosure was 20 deep, basking in the glory of a feat that will not be repeated in our lifetime. **SD**

Frankie Dettori shouts in triumph as Fujiyama Crest gives him his seventh winner of the day from seven rides

Press Association / Empics

Getty Images

Richard Dunwoody punches the air as Miinnehoma withstands the challenge of the gallant Just So

96

Miinnehoma's National

Grand National, Aintree, April 9, 1994

1. **Miinnehoma** 16-1
2. **Just So** 20-1
3. **Moorcroft Boy** 5-1f

Winning owner Freddie Starr **Trainer** Martin Pipe **Jockey** Richard Dunwoody **Distances** 1¼l, 20l

What made it great Still on the bridle after the last in the National? It was unheard of, but that was the situation Dunwoody and Miinnehoma found themselves in. Miinnehoma, carrying 10st 8lb, looked to have the race at his mercy with four to jump and was cantering in third as Moorcroft Boy led over the last two. Dunwoody even had the reserves and the audacity to take a pull on the run to the elbow, not wanting his mount to be left in front for too long. He led a furlong out, whereupon the dour stayer Just So threw down a challenge and got to Miinnehoma's girths, but his lack of acceleration proved decisive and Miinnehoma held on grimly to beat 'Just Slow'. **SD**

Mirrorpix

97

Lammtarra's Arc

Prix de l'Arc de Triomphe, Longchamp, October 1, 1995

1. **Lammtarra** 21-10f
2. **Freedom Cry** 64-10
3. **Swain** 22-10

Winning owner Godolphin/Saeed Maktoum Al Maktoum **Trainer** Saeed Bin Suroor **Jockey** Frankie Dettori **Distances** ³⁄₄l, 2l

What made it great An admirably courageous champion, Lammtarra retired unbeaten after an unforgettable autumn afternoon in Paris when he emulated Mill Reef to become only the second horse to complete Europe's ultimate middle-distance treble: Derby, King George and Arc. The Godolphin colt, who had overcome a life-threatening lung infection to win the Derby on his seasonal debut, possessed no real turn of foot, but, boy, could he gallop – and he had to at Longchamp, where Frankie Dettori went into overdrive after sending him on turning for home. Lammtarra was relentless, finding tremendous reserves to hold off Freedom Cry, who headed him within the final furlong. Brave indeed, and fully meriting the cheers instigated by his showman rider as he paraded the trophy in front of stands packed with British visitors. **NG**

Lammtarra (near side) is at full stretch to regain the lead from Freedom Cry in the last half-furlong

98

Generous's second Derby demolition

Irish Derby, The Curragh, June 30, 1991

1. **Generous** evens f
2. **Suave Dancer** 9-4
3. **Star Of Gdansk** 12-1

Winning owner Fahd Salman **Trainer** Paul Cole **Jockey** Alan Munro **Distances** 3l, 8l

What made it great Generous proved himself a great champion with this barnstorming defeat of an outstanding rival. The bright chestnut son of Caerleon had trounced his Epsom rivals by five lengths and the clash with Prix du Jockey-Club winner Suave Dancer – who had won his Classic by four lengths – was the highlight of the summer. Munro's plan was to extinguish Suave Dancer's brilliant turn of foot, and to that end he sent Generous on with more than a mile to run. The tactics worked and Generous barrelled through the last quarter-mile for a comprehensive success; Suave Dancer could never land a blow but gained his revenge in the Arc. **SD**

Generous has the race to himself as his forcing tactics prove decisive at The Curragh

Gerry and Mark Cranham

99

Eclipse first, the rest nowhere

Noblemen and Gentlemen's Plate, Epsom, May 3, 1769

1. **Eclipse** 1-4f
2. **Gower**
3. **Chance**

Winning owner William Wildman **Jockey** John Oakley

What made it great At the age of five, Eclipse made a spectacular start to the unbeaten 18-race career that made him the greatest champion of the 18th century. In a race run in four-mile heats at Epsom (this was 11 years before the inaugural Derby), he won the first heat, and in the second 'distanced' all his four rivals – i.e. eliminated them by beating them by more than 240 yards. Dennis O'Kelly, his subsequent owner, bet that he could name all the finishers in the correct order, and won by uttering the immortal words "Eclipse first and the rest nowhere". **JR**

Eclipse on his own – just like at Epsom when he distanced his rivals

Getty Images

100

Commanche Run and Piggott's record

St Leger, Doncaster, September 15, 1984

1. **Commanche Run** 7-4f
2. **Baynoun** 5-2
3. **Alphabatim** 7-1

Winning owner Ivan Allan **Trainer** Luca Cumani **Jockey** Lester Piggott **Distances** nk, 1½l

What made it great Commanche Run, in front all the way up Doncaster's long, strength-sapping straight, bravely lasted home under a coaxing Piggott ride, one in sharp contrast to his Derby wins on Roberto and The Minstrel. It looked as if Baynoun, under Steve Cauthen, could go past him at any point he wanted inside the last quarter-mile, but Piggott kept asking for a little more and Commanche Run kept finding it. It was a superb effort from a colt whose best wins the following season would be gained over ten furlongs, and it gave his rider the Classic success he needed – his 28th – to pass Frank Buckle's long-standing record. **SD**

Commanche Run keeps Baynoun at bay after an exhilarating battle in the final quarter-mile

Gerry and Mark Cranham

complete **votes**

A TOTAL of 273 races received at least one vote in the *Racing Post*'s quest to discover the 100 Greatest Races and, ultimately, the greatest of them all.

Here we list them all chronologically by year and, within each year, by number of votes. The prevalence of races that took place since the turn of the century seems to provide evidence for the newest memory being the brightest, and it would be interesting to see how many of the races from the last five years would figure in a poll conducted ten years hence.

However, greatness is permanent, as perhaps demonstrated by nine of the top ten races – and 14 of the top 20 – being more than 15 years old. Races were eligible by dint of their including a British- or Irish-trained runner. For example, Arazi's Breeders' Cup Juvenile triumph qualifies for the purposes of this poll only because of the presence of Showbrook, trained by Richard Hannon.

1769 Noblemen & Gentlemen's Plate, Epsom **Eclipse**
1799 Match at Newmarket **Hambletonian**
1851 Match at York **The Flying Dutchman**
1866 Gold Cup **Gladiateur**
1867 Derby **Hermit**
1886 2,000 Guineas **Ormonde**
     Derby **Ormonde**
1896 Derby **Persimmon**
1903 Eclipse Stakes **Ard Patrick**
1913 Derby **Aboyeur**
     Maiden Stakes, Newmarket **The Tetrarch**
1933 Derby **Hyperion**
1934 Cheltenham Gold Cup **Golden Miller**
1949 Ascot Gold Cup **Alycidon**
     Derby **Nimbus**
1953 Derby **Pinza**
1956 Prix de l'Arc de Triomphe **Ribot**
     King George VI and Queen Elizabeth Stakes **Ribot**
1958 Hennessy Gold Cup **Taxidermist**
1959 Oaks **Petite Étoile**
1961 Whitbread Gold Cup **Pas Seul**
1962 Grand Steeple-Chase de Paris **Mandarin**
     Oaks **Monade**
     News of the World Handicap **Tamerlo**
1964 Cheltenham Gold Cup **Arkle**
     Massey-Ferguson Gold Cup **Flying Wild**
     Grand National **Team Spirit**
     Lincolnshire Handicap **Mighty Gurkha**
1965 Prix de l'Arc de Triomphe **Sea-Bird**
     Gallaher Gold Cup **Arkle**
     St Leger **Provoke**
     Cheltenham Gold Cup **Arkle**
1966 Hennessy Gold Cup **Stalbridge Colonist**
     Champion Stakes **Pieces Of Eight**

1967 Grand National **Foinavon**
1968 Eclipse Stakes **Royal Palace**
     Derby **Sir Ivor**
     King George VI and Queen Elizabeth Stakes **Royal Palace**
1969 Prix de l'Arc de Triomphe **Levmoss**
1970 St Leger **Nijinsky**
     King George VI and Queen Elizabeth Stakes **Nijinsky**
     Champion Hurdle **Persian War**
1971 2,000 Guineas **Brigadier Gerard**
     Prix de l'Arc de Triomphe **Mill Reef**
     Grand National **Specify**
     Champion Hurdle **Bula**
     Derby **Mill Reef**
     St James's Palace Stakes **Brigadier Gerard**
1972 Derby **Roberto**
     Benson & Hedges Gold Cup **Roberto**
     King George VI and Queen Elizabeth Stakes **Brigadier Gerard**
     Sussex Stakes **Sallust**
     Cheltenham Gold Cup **Glencaraig Lady**
     Lincoln Cup point-to-point **Zendeal**
1973 Grand National **Red Rum**
     Cheltenham Gold Cup **The Dikler**
     King George VI and Queen Elizabeth Stakes **Dahlia**
1974 Champion Hurdle **Lanzarote**
     Cheltenham Gold Cup **Captain Christy**
     Triumph Hurdle **Attivo**
     Queen Anne Stakes **Brook**
1975 King George VI and Queen Elizabeth Diamond Stakes **Grundy**
     King George VI Chase **Captain Christy**
     St Leger **Bruni**
     Derby **Grundy**

1977 Templegate Hurdle **Night Nurse/Monksfield**
Grand National **Red Rum**
Derby **The Minstrel**
St Leger **Dunfermline**
King George VI and Queen Elizabeth Diamond
Stakes **The Minstrel**
Champion Hurdle **Night Nurse**
1978 Champion Hurdle **Monksfield**
Supreme Novices' Hurdle **Golden Cygnet**
Derby **Shirley Heights**
King George VI and Queen Elizabeth Diamond
Stakes **Ile de Bourbon**
1979 Champion Hurdle **Monksfield**
Derby **Troy**
Ebor Handicap **Sea Pigeon**
Embassy Premier Chase Final **Silver Buck**
Irish 2,000 Guineas **Dickens Hill**
Cheltenham Gold Cup **Alverton**
1980 Champion Hurdle **Sea Pigeon**
Ascot Gold Cup **Le Moss**
Queen Elizabeth II Stakes **Known Fact**
Cheltenham Gold Cup **Master Smudge**
Cheveley Park Stakes **Marwell**
1981 Grand National **Aldaniti**
Derby **Shergar**
Champion Hurdle **Sea Pigeon**
Cambridgeshire **Braughing**
Scottish National **Astral Charmer**
1982 Schweppes Gold Trophy **Donegal Prince**
Derby **Golden Fleece**
1983 Cheltenham Gold Cup **Bregawn**
Grand National **Corbiere**
Sun Alliance Novices' Hurdle **Sabin du Loir**
Horse and Hound Cup **Otter Way**
1984 Whitbread Gold Cup **Special Cargo**
2,000 Guineas **El Gran Senor**
Derby **Secreto**
Arkle Challenge Trophy **Bobsline**
St Leger **Commanche Run**
Hennessy Cognac Gold Cup **Burrough Hill Lad**
Cheltenham Gold Cup **Burrough Hill Lad**
Queen Elizabeth II Stakes **Teleprompter**
Ladbroke Novices' Hurdle Final **Run Over**
1985 1,000 Guineas **Oh So Sharp**
King George VI and Queen Elizabeth Diamond
Stakes **Petoski**
Champion Stakes **Pebbles**
Derby **Slip Anchor**
Breeders' Cup Turf **Pebbles**
Prix de l'Arc de Triomphe **Rainbow Quest**
1986 Prix de l'Arc de Triomphe **Dancing Brave**
Cheltenham Gold Cup **Dawn Run**
Derby **Shahrastani**
King George VI and Queen Elizabeth Diamond
Stakes **Dancing Brave**
Match at Punchestown **Dawn Run**

1987 Eclipse Stakes **Mtoto**
Breeders' Cup Mile **Miesque**
Cheltenham Gold Cup **The Thinker**
Champion Hurdle **See You Then**
1988 Grand National **Rhyme 'N' Reason**
King George VI and Queen Elizabeth Diamond
Stakes **Mtoto**
Whitbread Gold Cup **Desert Orchid**
1989 Cheltenham Gold Cup **Desert Orchid**
Victor Chandler Chase **Desert Orchid**
2,000 Guineas **Nashwan**
Racing Post Chase **Bonanza Boy**
King George VI and Queen Elizabeth Diamond
Stakes **Nashwan**
Queen Elizabeth II Stakes **Zilzal**
Black & White Whisky Champion Chase **Maid
Of Money**
1990 Breeders' Cup Mile **Royal Academy**
Nunthorpe Stakes **Dayjur**
Queen Mother Champion Chase **Barnbrook
Again**
Cheltenham Gold Cup **Norton's Coin**
King George VI Chase **Desert Orchid**
Grand National **Mr Frisk**
Breeders' Cup Sprint **Safely Kept**
Haydock Sprint Cup **Dayjur**
Lincoln Handicap **Amenable**
1991 Breeders' Cup Juvenile **Arazi**
1992 Sussex Stakes **Marling**
Cheltenham Gold Cup **Cool Ground**
Irish Champion Stakes **Dr Devious**
Sun Alliance Novices' Chase **Miinnehoma**
2,000 Guineas **Rodrigo de Triano**
King George VI and Queen Elizabeth Diamond
Stakes **St Jovite**
1993 King George VI Chase **Barton Bank**
Aintree Hurdle **Morley Street**
King George Stakes **Lochsong**
2,000 Guineas **Zafonic**
Melbourne Cup **Vintage Crop**
Scottish National **Run For Free**
Prix de l'Abbaye **Lochsong**
Grand National (void race)
1994 Queen Mother Champion Chase **Viking Flagship**
Grand National **Miinnehoma**
Breeders' Cup Mile **Barathea**
Derby **Erhaab**
Champion Hurdle **Flakey Dove**
Racing Post Trophy **Celtic Swing**
1995 Melling Chase **Viking Flagship**
Prix de l'Arc de Triomphe **Lammtarra**
Goodwood Cup **Double Trigger**
Derby **Lammtarra**
King George VI and Queen Elizabeth Diamond
Stakes **Lammtarra**
1996 Gordon Carter Handicap **Fujiyama Crest**

King George VI Chase **One Man**
Prix de l'Arc de Triomphe **Helissio**
Scottish National **Moorcroft Boy**
Oaks **Lady Carla**
2,000 Guineas **Mark Of Esteem**
Champion Stakes **Bosra Sham**
Royal Hunt Cup **Yeast**

1997 King George VI and Queen Elizabeth Diamond
Stakes **Swain**
Derby **Benny The Dip**
Goodwood Cup **Double Trigger**
Prince of Wales's Stakes **Bosra Sham**
Dubai World Cup **Singspiel**
Prix de l'Arc de Triomphe **Peintre Celebre**
Ascot Gold Cup **Celeric**
Champion Hurdle **Make A Stand**
Royal SunAlliance Novices' Hurdle **Istabraq**
Tingle Creek Trophy **Ask Tom**
Stayers' Hurdle **Karshi**
Peter Marsh Chase **Jodami**

1998 Queen Mother Champion Chase **One Man**
Aintree Hurdle **Pridwell**
Champion Hurdle **Istabraq**
Grand National **Earth Summit**
Goodwood Cup **Double Trigger**
Cheltenham Gold Cup **Cool Dawn**
Scottish National **Baronet**
Whitbread Gold Cup **Call It A Day**

1999 Prix de l'Arc de Triomphe **Montjeu**
Cheltenham Gold Cup **See More Business**
Breeders' Cup Turf **Daylami**
Irish Champion Stakes **Daylami**
King George VI Chase **See More Business**
July Cup **Stravinsky**
Queen Mother Champion Chase **Call Equiname**
St Leger **Mutafaweq**
Tingle Creek Trophy **Viking Flagship**

2000 Queen Mother Champion Chase **Edredon Bleu**
Dubai World Cup **Dubai Millennium**
Breeders' Cup Classic **Tiznow**
King George VI and Queen Elizabeth Diamond
Stakes **Montjeu**
Champion Hurdle **Istabraq**
Prince of Wales's Stakes **Dubai Millennium**
Eclipse Stakes **Giant's Causeway**
Irish Champion Stakes **Giant's Causeway**
St James's Palace Stakes **Giant's Causeway**
Prix de l'Arc de Triomphe **Sinndar**
Cheltenham Gold Cup **Looks Like Trouble**
Derby **Sinndar**
Navan Racing To Please You Chase **Nick Dundee**

2001 Irish Champion Stakes **Fantastic Light**
Breeders' Cup Classic **Tiznow**
King George VI and Queen Elizabeth Diamond
Stakes **Galileo**

Grand National **Red Marauder**
Breeders' Cup Turf **Fantastic Light**
Hennessy Cognac Gold Cup **Whats Up Boys**
Cleeve Hurdle **Lady Rebecca**
Coronation Stakes **Banks Hill**
Derby **Galileo**

2002 Doncaster Cup **Boreas**
Cheltenham Gold Cup **Best Mate**
Breeders' Cup Mile **Domedriver**
Prix du Moulin **Rock Of Gibraltar**
Champion Hurdle **Hors La Loi**
Queen Mother Champion Chase **Flagship
Uberalles**
2,000 Guineas **Rock Of Gibraltar**
Tripleprint Novices' Hurdle **Iris's Gift**
Ascot Hurdle **Istabraq**
Supreme Novices' Hurdle **Like-A-Butterfly**

2003 Breeders' Cup Turf **High Chaparral/Johar**
Jockey Club Cup **Persian Punch**
Goodwood Cup **Persian Punch**
Lockinge Stakes **Hawk Wing**
Cheltenham Gold Cup **Best Mate**
Queen Elizabeth II Stakes **Falbrav**
Becher Chase **Clan Royal**
Stayers' Hurdle **Baracouda**
Champion Hurdle **Rooster Booster**
Kingwell Hurdle **Rhinestone Cowboy**
Hennessy Cognac Gold Cup **Strong Flow**
Irish Champion Stakes **High Chaparral**
1,000 Guineas **Russian Rhythm**
Irish Champion Hurdle **Like-A-Butterfly**
Queen Anne Stakes **Dubai Destination**
Paddy Power Future Champions Novice Hurdle
Mariah Rollins
Coral.co.uk Handicap Chase **Kingscliff**
Esher Stakes **Persian Punch**

2004 Cheltenham Gold Cup **Best Mate**
Tingle Creek Trophy **Moscow Flyer**
Stayers' Hurdle **Iris's Gift**
Victor Chandler Chase **Isio**
Grand National **Amberleigh House**
Champion Stakes **Haafhd**
Sussex Stakes **Soviet Song**
Supreme Novices' Hurdle **Brave Inca**
Irish Champion Stakes **Azamour**
Queen Anne Stakes **Refuse To Bend**
Irish St Leger **Vinnie Roe**
Lockinge Stakes **Russian Rhythm**
Falmouth Stakes **Soviet Song**
Champion Hurdle **Hardy Eustace**
Breeders' Cup Juvenile **Wilko**
Long Walk Hurdle **Baracouda**
Christmas Hurdle **Harchibald**
Matron Stakes **Soviet Song**
Vodafone Dash **Caribbean Coral**
Pertemps Handicap Hurdle Qualifier **Quick**

statistical **breakdown**

THE quest to discover the identity of the greatest race ever run in Britain and Ireland took two months, although it can equally be said that the search for the greatest race is an ongoing and infinite one. Next year might bring us a new no.1.

Votes came cascading into the *Racing Post* office and the list of the top 100 greatest races – voted for by *Post* readers and a panel of *Post* experts – was gradually compiled.

There were many surprises along the way, and many occasions when a first-choice vote left us staring into the middle distance, transported back to the nip-and-tuck of a mighty duel of the past.

Many nominations waxed eloquently in support of a particular race, and rightly so. Our favourite voter, though, went for brevity in an attempt to convey his feelings. His email read simply: "Arkle". The great horse always was a race apart.

Two years ago *Racing Post* readers had been asked to choose their 100 Racing Greats, a poll eventually topped by legendary trainer Vincent O'Brien. Last year the 100 favourite horses ever to run in Britain and Ireland were chosen, and Arkle was the number one.

For this poll, the rules were simple. Any race staged in Britain and Ireland was eligible, plus any race anywhere in the world as long as it included a British- or Irish-trained horse.

Readers voted for their greatest races in 1-2-3 order, with their first choice awarded more points than their second and their second choice more than their third.

Amberleigh House takes the fourth-last alongside previous winner Monty's Pass in the 2004 Grand National – voted the ninth-greatest Aintree race

Getty Images

TOP TEN JUMP RACES

1989 Cheltenham Gold Cup (Desert Orchid)

1973 Grand National (Red Rum)

1986 Cheltenham Gold Cup (Dawn Run)

1964 Cheltenham Gold Cup (Arkle)

1984 Whitbread Gold Cup (Special Cargo)

1977 Templegate Hurdle (Night Nurse/Monksfield)

1977 Grand National (Red Rum)

1981 Grand National (Aldaniti)

1995 Melling Chase (Viking Flagship)

2000 Queen Mother Champion Chase (Edredon Bleu)

TOP TEN FLAT RACES

1975 King George VI and Queen Elizabeth Diamond Stakes (Grundy)

1986 Prix de l'Arc de Triomphe (Dancing Brave)

2001 Irish Champion Stakes (Fantastic Light)

1990 Breeders' Cup Mile (Royal Academy)

2003 Breeders' Cup Turf (High Chaparral/Johar)

1971 2,000 Guineas (Brigadier Gerard)

1972 Derby (Roberto)

1991 Breeders' Cup Juvenile (Arazi)

1965 Prix de l'Arc de Triomphe (Sea-Bird)

2003 Jockey Club Cup (Persian Punch)

TOP TEN RACES OUTSIDE BRITAIN AND IRELAND

1986 Prix de l'Arc de Triomphe (Dancing Brave)

1990 Breeders' Cup Mile (Royal Academy)

2003 Breeders' Cup Turf (High Chaparral/Johar)

1991 Breeders' Cup Juvenile (Arazi)

1965 Prix de l'Arc de Triomphe (Sea-Bird)

2000 Dubai World Cup (Dubai Millennium)

1962 Grand Steeple-Chase de Paris (Mandarin)

2001 Breeders' Cup Classic (Tiznow)

2000 Breeders' Cup Classic (Tiznow)

1971 Prix de l'Arc de Triomphe (Mill Reef)

TOP TEN DERBYS

1972 Roberto

1913 Aboyeur

1981 Shergar

1977 The Minstrel

1984 Secreto

1979 Troy

1997 Benny The Dip

1965 Sea-Bird

1968 Sir Ivor

1867 Hermit

TOP TEN RACES WON BY FILLIES OR MARES

1986 Cheltenham Gold Cup (Dawn Run)

1985 1,000 Guineas (Oh So Sharp)

1992 Sussex Stakes (Marling)

1964 Massey-Ferguson Gold Cup (Flying Wild)

1977 St Leger (Dunfermline)

1985 Champion Stakes (Pebbles)

1936 Ascot Gold Cup (Quashed)

1972 Cheltenham Gold Cup (Glencaraig Lady)

1985 Breeders' Cup Turf (Pebbles)

2002 Supreme Novices' Hurdle (Like-A-Butterfly)

TOP TEN GRAND NATIONALS

1973 Red Rum

1977 Red Rum

1981 Aldaniti

1967 Foinavon

1956 E.S.B. (Devon Loch)

1988 Rhyme 'N' Reason

1971 Specify

1994 Miinnehoma

2004 Amberleigh House

1983 Corbiere

TOP TEN RACES AT CHELTENHAM FESTIVAL

1989 Gold Cup (Desert Orchid)

1986 Gold Cup (Dawn Run)

1964 Gold Cup (Arkle)

2000 Queen Mother Champion Chase (Edredon Bleu)

1983 Gold Cup (Bregawn)

1980 Champion Hurdle (Sea Pigeon)

2004 Gold Cup (Best Mate)

1998 Queen Mother Champion Chase (One Man)

1984 Arkle Challenge Trophy (Bobsline)

1990 Queen Mother Champion Chase (Barnbrook Again)

Extra weighting was given to races run prior to 1970, and slightly more to races run before 1960.

Votes were cast for a smattering of races from the 19th century and the early 20th century, but the vast majority were for races from 1960 onwards, the era of television and wider media coverage. It may also say something about the age of the average *Racing Post* reader!

Only 15 races staged before 1950 received votes; and it has to be said that most of those were voted for by the *Racing Post* panel. Conversely, 70 races from the five eligible years of this century collected votes, and it will be interesting to see how many retain their hold on the public consciousness in, say, ten years' time. It's been said that propinquity is the greatest aphrodisiac; the love for, for example, the 2003 1,000 Guineas may not be a lasting one.

Many of the top 100 were obvious choices; it seems that for a race to be considered great, it has to take place on a major stage. Thirsk handicaps and Fakenham maiden hurdles are evidently not endowed with greatness.

While many races attracted either a few votes or a landslide, there were some whose score – surprisingly – resolutely remained at zero. Votes were cast, for example, for the 1975 Derby (won by Grundy) and the 2001 Derby (Galileo), but not for the 1989 Derby (Nashwan) or the 1982 renewal (Golden Fleece).

Why did the 1995 Cheltenham Gold Cup, won by Master Oats, fail to garner even a solitary third-placed vote, while See More Business' victory in the same race four years later was ranked as high as 79th place?

Some horses are conspicuous by their absence from the list. In the case of Baracouda and Soviet Song, however, it certainly wasn't down to the fact that they had failed to win a race deemed great. Quite the reverse; if all the votes for either horse had been directed at a single race, then that race would certainly have made the final 100. However, votes were spread too thinly among several stirring contests won by the pair and, as a result, you will search in vain for any of their victories. although Baracouda's defeat at the 2004 Cheltenham Festival made it to no.74.

There were some surprises. Why was the 2002 Doncaster Cup, won by Boreas, as high as no.54 on the list? It was an exciting contest, doubtless, but a greater race than the much-hyped 2004 Tingle Creek Trophy, or Sir Ivor's Derby, or Mill House's Whitbread Gold Cup? Were you sure?

The inclusion of the 1967 Grand National, won by Foinavon, led to some spluttering from several members of the panel on the grounds that it was "a dreadful race", but *Post* readers considered it great so in it went at no.21.

All steps were taken to turn aside any attempts at ballot-rigging, any attempts to skew such an important poll and therefore attempt to rewrite history. There was no funny business until the closing stages of the poll, when votes started to arrive by the barrowload for the 1990 Queen Mother Champion Chase, won narrowly by Barnbrook Again from Waterloo Boy.

The first few emails were diligently counted, even though there was only one race nominated, no 1-2-3. The individualities of the general public must occasionally be indulged.

Suspicions were aroused, however, when on the final afternoon for voting, every other email seemed to be identically worded in favour of the 1990 Champion Chase. No 1-2-3, just a plea for Barnbrook Again's finest hour to be top of the pile.

Several of those emails appeared to emanate from a similar source – it was as if a tap, or possibly a faucet, had been turned on. (You know who you are.) Collusion? Coincidence? It all seemed rather undemocratic. Those later votes, we must confess, had no influence whatsoever on the finishing position of the 1990 Champion Chase – though it still made no.53!

The top ten, the *crème de la crème* of all the uncountable races run over the last 300 years or so, were pretty much what had been expected. Some things should never change. The odometer of greatness was turned back to zero and the voting began again.

The 1977 Templegate Hurdle received just five per cent of the final vote, with the 1990 Breeders' Cup Mile, the 1984 Whitbread Gold Cup and the 2001 Irish Champion Stakes only a percentage point more favoured.

The next five places were closely contested – there were just four percentage points between the 1964 Cheltenham Gold Cup, the 1986 Cheltenham Gold Cup, the 1986 Prix de l'Arc de Triomphe, the 1975 King George VI and Queen Elizabeth Diamond Stakes and the 1973 Grand National.

It may have come as a surprise to some that the great contest between the freewheeling Crisp and the stalking Red Rum was only second, but with 14 per cent of the vote even the Aintree legends had to play second fiddle to the great grey and the horse who almost spoiled the party – for it takes two to make a horse race. The 1989 Cheltenham Gold Cup garnered 16 per cent of the vote, a clear majority.

But one thing should be remembered. The 1989 Cheltenham Gold Cup was not great just because Desert Orchid won it. No race merits the accolade of greatness purely for the identity of the winner. The race didn't even see Desert Orchid's greatest performance – the win was officially rated 13lb below his best.

But it was, indisputably, a great race – the kind of race that, years from now, people will be able to recall exactly where they were when Desert Orchid dug impossibly deep to see off the equally brave Yahoo in conditions that were practically unraceable.

Many factors made it a great race; you made it the greatest.

ireland's top ten

The Racing Post's Irish correspondent
Tony O'Hehir lists his nation's finest races

1 2003 Irish Champion Stakes
High Chaparral

For obvious reasons, Ireland's highest-rated Flat race was always going to contribute handsomely to this personal list, and the 2003 running of the Irish Champion Stakes stands out as arguably the best of all.

It had plenty going for it to justify that claim. A top-class international field of high achievers including Falbrav, who had won the Eclipse Stakes and the Juddmonte International, Alamshar, the Irish Derby and King George VI and Queen Elizabeth Diamond Stakes winner, Moon Ballad, winner of that year's Dubai World Cup, and Islington, winner of the Yorkshire Oaks, took on High Chaparral who, as part of a new policy by the Coolmore-Ballydoyle team, had been kept in training to build on his achievements as a three-year-old, which saw him complete the Epsom-Curragh Derby double and win the Breeders' Cup Turf.

Less than two lengths covered the first four, all of whom were Group 1 winners, at the finish of a race run in a fast time. And it all had an element of controversy and a long-running sequel that involved a stewards' inquiry, an objection and an appeal, none of which led to any change in the result.

High Chaparral, who would go on to achieve a second Breeders' Cup Turf win later that season, emerged victorious with a gutsy display that confirmed him as a performer of the highest class. Mick Kinane rode a fine tactical race on the winner, striking the front a furlong out and getting first run on Falbrav, on whom Darryll Holland elected to go the inside route, only to find himself short of room as High Chaparral edged to the left.

A neck divided High Chaparral and Falbrav at the finish, with Islington, who went on to land the Breeders' Cup Filly and Mare Turf at Santa Anita, a head back in third.

2 2001 Irish Champion Stakes
Fantastic Light

The clash between Galileo and Fantastic Light in the King George VI and Queen Elizabeth Diamond Stakes had been the highlight of the summer. This was even better, with Frankie Dettori and Fantastic Light slipping through on the inside to hit the front off the final bend, getting first run on Galileo and Mick Kinane. The Ballydoyle colt arrived alongside Fantastic Light early in the final furlong and lost out by only a head as they went to the line locked in battle.

3 2005 Irish Champion Hurdle
Macs Joy

A race that produced a finish more in keeping with a big sprint handicap run in mid-summer, but this was heavy ground with a capital H and Macs Joy, Brave Inca and Hardy Eustace, all of them Grade 1 winners, served up a cracking finish with only a short head and a head separating them at the line. Hardy Eustace was to gain his revenge when successfully defending his Champion Hurdle crown at Cheltenham two months later. However, while he lost this particular race, there were really no losers in as exciting a finish to a jump race as I can recall.

4 1986 Punchestown match
Dawn Run

In a flashback to olden times, this match race between two high-class, and hugely popular, chasers caught the imagination, coming as it did a month after both had won at the Cheltenham Festival, Dawn Run in the Gold Cup and Buck House in the Champion Chase. They met at level weights with Tony Mullins back on 'the mare' after losing the ride in the Gold Cup to Jonjo O'Neill. Tommy Carmody and Buck House put it up to the 4-6 favourite, but Dawn Run emerged victorious by two and a half lengths. Both these fine champions were lost within a few months of this encounter; Dawn Run was killed in the French Champion Hurdle while Buck House died after becoming a victim of colic while out at grass.

5 2003 Irish Derby Alamshar

Both leading contenders were bred and owned by the Aga Khan. Dalakhani had won the Prix du Jockey-Club and started 4-7 favourite. Alamshar had been third in the Derby and was 4-1 second best in the market. Local knowledge played a big part in the outcome, as Johnny Murtagh's experience of The Curragh and Christophe Soumillon's lack of it was, unquestionably, a factor in Alamshar achieving a dramatic half-length win over his French-trained rival.

6 1991 Irish Derby Generous

The race brought together two outstanding Derby winners in Generous, the Epsom hero, and Suave Dancer, who had outclassed his rivals at Chantilly. Suave Dancer was to finish the season the better, with Group 1 wins in the Irish Champion Stakes and the Prix de l'Arc de Triomphe, but at The Curragh Generous was on a roll – he was to go on and land the King George – and under a positive, attacking ride from Alan Munro he saw off John Hammond's colt by three lengths.

7 2000 Irish Champion Stakes Giant's Causeway

The one they called 'the Iron Horse' got the chance to display his battling qualities when recording his fifth straight Group 1 win of the season and his only Group 1 success in Ireland. His way of doing things was the hard way and, after taking the lead entering the straight, he did little enough in front before responding gamely to hold off the late charge of Greek Dance by half a length. His never-say-die attitude made him more popular with many Irish racegoers than other more flamboyant Group 1 horses, and he returned to the type of rousing reception one associates more with the jumping game.

8 2003 Irish Champion Hurdle Like-A-Butterfly

Limestone Lad, the most popular jumper in Ireland in the early years of the new millennium, was more effective over two and a half or three miles. However, the Bowe family's hero, winner of 35 of his 65 races, knew only one way of racing – from the front – and he tried to burn off his four rivals over a trip short of his best. Like-A-Butterfly jumped past him at the last, but Limestone Lad came back for more and was only a head behind at the line.

9 1992 Irish Derby St Jovite

Excuses were made for the Derby winner Dr Devious, but St Jovite was truly awesome in trouncing that rival, and the rest, by 12 lengths, the biggest winning margin in the history of the race. Victory in the King George was to follow for Jim Bolger's colt, before Dr Devious made it 2-1 in their head-to-head meetings by pipping St Jovite in the Irish Champion Stakes.

10 1991 Irish 2,000 Guineas Fourstars Allstar

The reason for its place on this list is twofold: a thrilling finish and, more importantly, the significance of the result in the long history of Irish racing. Fourstars Allstar, ridden by Mike Smith, became the first horse trained in the US to win an Irish Classic, and made the occasion a special one for his Irish-American trainer Leo O'Brien. A head separated the winner and Star Of Gdansk at the finish, with six lengths back to the third, Lycius.

france's top ten

 French correspondent **Desmond Stoneham** with ten of the best from across the Channel

1 1962 Grand Steeple-Chase de Paris Mandarin

As many of my top ten are covered in detail elsewhere in this book, I have concentrated on those lower down my list that make their only appearance here.

However, I must say rather more about my number one, a race that was marked by an unforgettable performance from both horse and rider and thus wins my vote as the greatest in the history of French racing.

The Fulke Walwyn-trained Mandarin had to overcome serious injury problems well before he arrived in Paris in June 1962 for his final race, the dual King George winner having battled back from serious leg problems sustained when falling in the 1958 Cheltenham Gold Cup.

However, Mandarin had already won both the Hennessy and the Gold Cup itself during the 1961/62 season before he was sent over the Channel to contest France's championship steeplechase. What followed beggared belief, thanks to an extraordinary effort from Fred Winter in the saddle on the bravest and most willing of partners.

There were still 25 challenging fences to cross when Mandarin's bit snapped after the third, leaving Winter with no steering. For seven minutes and the best part of three and a half miles, Winter fought to keep the partnership intact.

Able to guide Mandarin only by shifting his weight using his legs and arms, Winter somehow managed to point his mount around the twisting Auteuil course. Several French jockeys also showed tremendous sportsmanship in helping to keep the English visitor on course.

Steering proved to be only half the equation, though, for Mandarin bowed a tendon before the last and was, in effect, running on three legs after that. He held on to win by a head from Lumino in what was a towering achievement by both a fantastically skilled horseman and a remarkably courageous horse, who was retired after the race to become his trainer's hack.

2 1965 Arc de Triomphe Sea-Bird

An awesome individual, the Derby winner was outstanding when romping home from the most exalted field in Arc history. Despite veering left in the final furlong, he still trounced some immensely talented rivals including multiple top-level winners such as Reliance, Meadow Court and Tom Rolfe, winner of America's Preakness Stakes.

3 1956 Arc de Triomphe Ribot

Unbeaten in 16 starts, it was Ribot's second success in the Longchamp showpiece that left the most indelible impression. Pulverising his rivals in the straight, he fairly flew the last furlong and a half in the heavy ground to finish alone, the stunning six-length success over Talgo establishing a record margin that has never been surpassed.

4 1971 Arc de Triomphe Mill Reef

More than 53,000 racegoers descended on the Bois de Boulogne to see the great Mill Reef, sent off at odds-on under Geoff Lewis, outgun France's champion filly Pistol Packer. Mill Reef had the others cold by the furlong marker and went on to win by three lengths in record time.

5 1986 Arc de Triomphe
Dancing Brave

One of the greatest finishes in Arc history as Dancing Brave, to the delight of thousands of English visitors, achieved greatness by swooping from way back under Pat Eddery to conquer the Prix du Jockey-Club winner Bering. He, too, set a record time.

6 1939 Grand Prix de Paris
Pharis

The great unbeaten champion Pharis raced only three times, but his career included commanding performances in both the Prix du Jockey-Club and the Grand Prix de Paris in 1939. In the latter race he was bumped at the start and found himself unbalanced and shut in towards the back of the field. Apparently facing an impossible task in the straight, he flew like an arrow to the line once in the clear. Pharis was due to clash with Blue Peter, winner of the 2,000 Guineas and Derby, in the St Leger when war intervened. He never ran again.

7 1974 Arc de Triomphe
Allez France

Allez France won the French 1,000 Guineas and Oaks in 1973 but found the Arc beyond her when beaten two and a half lengths by the Derby runner-up Rheingold. Twelve months later, though, she made amends under multiple French champion jockey Yves Saint-Martin, who arrived at Longchamp on crutches, injuries to his thigh and back relieved only by pain-killing injections following a fall ten days earlier. The race itself was far from straightforward: Allez France saw daylight too early, seemingly making her a sitting duck in the straight. Nevertheless, she held on by a head from Comtesse de Loir, much to her rider's delight. "My beauty!" he exclaimed afterwards. "My star, my queen, my great love! You will always be with me in mind, body and soul. I suffered for you, you who gave me such great pleasure."

8 1984 Grand Prix de Saint-Cloud **Teenoso**

A performance above and beyond the call of duty from a blood-spattered Lester Piggott on the previous season's Derby winner, who whipped round in the pre-race parade, threw his head up and cut his rider's right eye. Piggott refused to see the racecourse doctor and went down to the start as normal. Once he put on his goggles, however, they filled with blood, with the result that he rode most of the race with extremely limited vision. It didn't stop him winning, though – and blood went all over Piggott's silks in the winner's enclosure.

9 1979 Prix Thomas Bryon
Nureyev

The son of Northern Dancer had made headlines almost from birth, having been knocked down to Greek shipping magnate Stavros Niarchos for $1.3m as a yearling in 1978, and at Saint-Cloud in October 1979 trainer François Boutin found out for certain that he had something special. Nureyev, ridden by Philippe Paquet, cantered home in this Group 3 contest by six lengths on his racecourse debut. Sadly, though, like Pharis, he was to race only three times. After being demoted from first place in the 2,000 Guineas, Nureyev was struck down by a virus while being prepared for the Derby and never had the chance to realise his full potential.

10 1997 Arc de Triomphe
Peintre Celebre

Shades of Sea-Bird as Peintre Celebre passed the post well clear of his rivals – and clipped 1.6 seconds off the track record into the bargain, establishing a mark that has yet to be bettered. The son of Nureyev won the Prix du Jockey-Club and the Grand Prix de Paris before the Arc, and his surprise defeat in the Prix Niel was due to some aggressive riding tactics employed by another jockey. He was capable of accelerating more than once in a race, though sadly a tendon injury meant he never raced as a four-year-old.

america's top ten

US correspondent **Dan Farley** recalls some remarkable Stateside contests

1 **1973 Belmont Stakes**
Secretariat

By the spring of 1973, no three-year-old had won the US Triple Crown, the Holy Grail of American racing, since Citation had accomplished the feat 25 years earlier. Hopes were high, though, for Secretariat, the big, athletic chestnut trained by Lucien Laurin who had stirred the imagination as a two-year-old, when his dominance over the division was enough to make him Horse of the Year, a rarity for a juvenile.

He did not disappoint in the races that mattered the following season. Secretariat broke the track record in the Kentucky Derby under regular partner Ron Turcotte with a mark of 1m 59.4s. He followed it up with a visually stunning performance in the Preakness, moving from last to first on the first turn and winning as he pleased.

Then came the final leg of the Triple Crown, the Belmont and a gruelling mile and a half round the wide oval circuit. Secretariat's reputation was sky-high by this time. He had been syndicated at a value of $6.08 million and had appeared on the cover of *Time*, *Newsweek* and *Sports Illustrated*. That day at Belmont, he earned his place in history.

Gates open and Secretariat, the 1-10 favourite, goes at it immediately with Sham – runner-up in both the Derby and the Preakness and top-class in his own right. Only a head separates them at halfway, after six furlongs in 1m 9.8s, ridiculously fast. Many in an on-track crowd of 67,605 and an estimated 30 million television audience are asking themselves what the hell those guys are doing – and soon Secretariat finds himself very much alone, his rival fracturing a leg.

Race caller Chic Anderson says: "Secretariat is blazing along. Secretariat is widening now. He is moving like a tremendous machine!" The horse known as 'Big Red' pulls ten lengths clear, 15 lengths, 18 lengths. Jaws drop; please, please, don't stop now.

Secretariat hits the midpoint of the stretch turn, three furlongs to run. There is no sign of a slowdown. At the top of the straight his lead is 23 lengths after ten furlongs in 1m 59s. That is 0.4s faster than his Derby time and a full second faster than any other ten furlongs run in the Belmont itself.

With half a furlong to run the teletimer becomes the focus of everyone's attention as Secretariat chases the Belmont record of 2m 26.6s. He not only catches it, he crushes it: his final time a remarkable 2min 24s and his winning margin an even more remarkable 31 lengths. It is a standard of greatness by which every subsequent runner in US racing will be judged, and we still await its equal.

2 **1978 Belmont Stakes** Affirmed

Affirmed and Alydar laid it on the line time after time, finishing first and second, in either order, on no fewer than nine of their ten meetings. Affirmed had gained the ascendancy, as he usually did, in both the Kentucky Derby and the Preakness under a youthful Steve Cauthen, and a Triple Crown on the line in the Belmont only heightened the stakes. Affirmed went to the front early and still held a slight lead entering the straight, then Alydar actually nosed ahead for a stride or two. But Cauthen reached back with his left hand and struck Affirmed, the horse responded like the champion he was, and the Triple Crown was his by a head.

Bob Coglianese/NYRA

**Secretariat first, the rest nowhere:
'Big Red' stuns the racing world with
a 31-length victory under Ron Turcotte**

Secretariat's Belmont

Belmont Park, New York, June 9, 1973
1 Secretariat 1-10f
2 Twice A Prince 16-1
3 My Gallant 11-1
Winning owner Meadow Stable
Trainer Lucien Laurin
Jockey Ron Turcotte
Distances 31l, ½l

3 1976 Marlboro Cup Forego

Belmont again as the massive Forego shouldered a colossal burden to a memorable success. The impost of 9st 11lb he was assigned for this top-class handicap is the sort of weight rarely carried in the US. It looked too much when, a furlong out, leading three-year-old Honest Pleasure (in receipt of 18lb) cruised on the lead. Forego was four lengths back but the old man kept rolling relentlessly and at the wire he had the call by a head.

4 1988 Breeders' Cup Distaff
Personal Ensign

In what was arguably the greatest Breeders' Cup race ever, not many would have given Personal Ensign any chance at the top of the straight. Even at the furlong marker it looked as if it would take a miracle for anyone to catch Kentucky Derby-winning filly Winning Colors, but Personal Ensign cut into her advantage with each stride and a final lunge got her home by the slimmest of margins, ending her career with a perfect record of 13 victories from 13 starts.

5 1978 Jockey Club Gold Cup
Exceller

Billed as the clash of the Triple Crown winners Affirmed and Seattle Slew, the former failed to figure after his saddle slipped. Seattle Slew laid down very fast fractions, thereby providing an ideal set-up for multiple Group/Grade 1 winner Exceller, who produced a stunning response when Bill Shoemaker asked him for his run up the rail. He collared the leader, yet Angel Cordero somehow got Seattle Slew to rally again. At the line it was Exceller by a short head.

6 1962 Travers Stakes Jaipur

A great duel for Saratoga's 'midsummer derby' in which Belmont winner Jaipur and Preakness runner-up Ridan raced stride for stride virtually all the way. At the top of the straight the odds-on Jaipur took a narrow lead, but his rival would concede nothing and was gaining with every stride nearing the wire. It went to Jaipur – by a short head.

7 1982 Santa Anita Handicap
John Henry

Horse of the Year John Henry made his seasonal debut in the prestigious Santa Anita Handicap, a race he had won the previous year. No horse had ever won the 'Big 'Cap' twice, and the immensely popular gelding's brave rally from a long way back came up a short head short of Perrault. However, the closing stages involved some serious bumping and John Henry was awarded the race.

8 1968 Washington Park
Handicap Dr. Fager

The brilliant Dr. Fager carved his name into history with this performance at Arlington. Under a huge burden of 9st 8lb, he blazed through the Washington Park's mile to win by ten lengths in 1m 32.2s, eclipsing the great Buckpasser's world record of 1m 32.6s. It was a mark that stood for 29 years.

9 1985 Breeders' Cup Turf
Pebbles

A race won in a manner that was testament to the courage of a truly admirable filly. Snatched up after the stretch turn, Pebbles, full of determination, renewed her effort twice – once to get to the lead at the furlong marker, and again to withstand Strawberry Road, who came flying at her late in the straight. Dubbed "England's superfilly" by the race caller, they didn't come any tougher.

10 1955 Kentucky Derby Swaps

Nashua was 13-10 favourite following three wins in the major trials, whereas Swaps had run only once beyond seven furlongs and had won over six furlongs at Churchill Downs the week before the Derby. It was hardly a conventional preparation, but Bill Shoemaker took Swaps to the lead at the start and never looked back, winning by a length and a half from his great rival.

australia's top ten

Australian correspondent **Syd Brennan** names his country's most memorable races

1 **1982 Cox Plate**
Kingston Town

Kingston Town's victory in Australia's premier weight-for-age event gets my vote. Greatness surrounded this horse, the outstanding galloper of his era and a champion in every sense of the word.

Trained by the legendary Tommy Smith – racing's equivalent of Don Bradman, who won 33 consecutive trainers' titles in Sydney between 1952-53 and 1984-85 and sent out more than 7,000 winners altogether – the big black gelding's career record was mightily impressive.

He won 30 of his 41 starts, including 21 consecutive races in Sydney, among them the AJC Derby and Sydney Cup in 1980, and 14 Group 1s. His Group wins included races at trips from 1,200 metres (six furlongs) to 3,200 metres (two miles) and he was the first Australian horse to reach $1 million in prize-money.

Though not entirely suited by the tight, turning Moonee Valley track, Kingston Town had won the two previous runnings of the race, joining an illustrious list of horses to win in successive years, following the great Phar Lap (1930-31), Young Idea (1936-37), Beau Vite (1940-41), Hydrogen (1952-53) and Tobin Bronze (1966-67). The feat has since been achieved by Sunline (1999-2000) and Northerly (2001-02).

The six-year-old was a hot favourite at 7-4 to complete the treble, but during the race not much went right for him and jockey Peter Cook, and coming to the home turn things didn't look rosy. The racecourse commentator was the late Bill Collins, known as 'The Accurate One' for his ability to correctly call

even the closest photo-finish. He said what everyone was thinking. "Kingston Town can't win," Collins told the huge crowd – but, for once, he was wrong.

After straightening for home Kingston Town somehow threaded his way through a gap and went after the leaders from a seemingly impossible position. Collins's tone changed. "He might get up yet, the champ," he said. "Kingston Town's swamping them . . ."

Once out into the open, with clear galloping room, the race was over in a matter of strides. It was an extraordinary feat – and an unforgettable performance.

2 **1982 Melbourne Cup**
Gurner's Lane

When Kingston Town lined up in the Melbourne Cup just ten days after his third Cox Plate success, the big question was whether he would get the two-mile trip. After straightening up for home, Malcolm Johnston angled the horse out and the crowd roared as he strode to the front. However, they had reckoned without Mick Dittman on Caulfield Cup winner Gurner's Lane, and 'The Enforcer' thrust his mount through gaps on the rails to nail Kingston Town in the closing stages. It was close enough that Tommy Smith, watching the race in the trainers' stand a furlong and a half from the winning post, threw his hands in the air, believing Kingston Town had won.

3 **1986 Cox Plate** Bonecrusher

Billed as a match between the two great New Zealanders Our Waverley Star and Bonecrusher, this exalted pair did not let anybody down with a titanic battle over the last half-

Melbourne Age

Kingston Town the third

WS Cox Plate, Moonee Valley, Melbourne, October 23, 1982

1 Kingston Town 7-4f

2 Grosvenor 13-2

3 My Axeman 6-1

Winning owners Mr & Mrs David Hains & GA Monsbourgh

Trainer Tommy Smith

Jockey Peter Cook

Distances ¾l, 1¼l

Kingston Town (arrowed) could never win from that position – oh yes he could, he 'swamped them'

mile. Locked together rounding the home turn, the pair seemed to be running on empty up the straight. Bonecrusher just held on, with Bill Collins again making a call that lives on in Cox Plate history. "Bonecrusher races into equine immortality," he said – and he was right.

4 1930 Melbourne Cup Phar Lap

No list would be complete without equine legend Phar Lap, the most popular horse in the history of Australian racing whose story became a feature film long before Seabiscuit. Phar Lap's Melbourne Cup was a race full of drama and intrigue. After track work at Caulfield four days before the Cup, an attempt was made on Phar Lap's life with a shotgun, after which he was taken to a secret hideout and taken to Flemington on raceday with a police escort, arriving just 40 minutes before post time. Despite this, and a massive burden of 9st 12lb, Phar Lap's supporters sent him off an 8-11 favourite. Never in danger of defeat, the giant chestnut cruised home by three lengths. No wonder he was a superstar.

5 2001 Cox Plate Northerly

West Australian champ Northerly spoiled the party for champion mare Sunline, who was attempting to emulate Kingston Town with her third Cox Plate in a row. She had her rivals off the bit turning for home, but Northerly was nothing if not a real trier. Responding to Damien Oliver's urgings, he collared the mare in the shadow of the post. Northerly won again the following year.

6 1997 Melbourne Cup Might And Power

Might And Power completed the Caulfield-Melbourne Cup double with a superb front-running display of sustained speed. Having won the first leg in comfortable fashion, he had to dig deep at the end of two miles in the Melbourne Cup to hold off Doriemus, winner of the race two years earlier.

7 1890 Melbourne Cup Carbine

A great weight-carrying performance from another equine legend in Carbine, who shouldered 10st 5lb to victory in a record field of 39 runners. 'Old Jack', as he was known, raced prominently throughout before a powerful finishing run carried him to the lead with less than a furlong to go. He won easily by two lengths. A year earlier Carbine carried 10st – a stone more than weight-for-age for a four-year-old – into second place.

8 1992 Stradbroke Handicap Rough Habit

New Zealand's Rough Habit won Queensland's richest sprint in 1991 and 1992, and his second victory was the finest. With a furlong to go he looked to have an impossible task with 12 horses in front of him, but he produced an amazing burst of speed that carried him to a memorable victory.

9 1991 Epsom Handicap Super Impose

Super Impose's second Epsom Handicap win over the metric mile at Randwick was something to behold. With his mount carrying 9st 8lb and in a seemingly impossible position on the home turn, jockey Darren Beadman angled for an inside run, remarkably getting up to win by more than a length from Livistona Lane. The crowd roared "Super, Super, Super!" when the pair returned to unsaddle.

10 1956 Hotham Handicap Ark Royal/Pandie Sun/Fighting Force

There are many others I could have picked, like Rain Lover's eight-length Melbourne Cup win in 1968 or Taj Rossi's astonishing performance in the George Adams Handicap (1973). But how can I leave out the first triple dead-heat after photo-finish cameras were installed in 1948? Three horses battled to the finish after a mile and a half and hit the line with not a breath separating them.

tony morris's top ten

The world's foremost bloodstock expert
with a personal selection

1 1965 Arc de Triomphe
Sea-Bird

The greatest racehorse of the last 80 years was Sea-Bird, and the greatest performance of the last 80 years was Sea-Bird's victory in the Prix de l'Arc de Triomphe.

Who says so? The late Quintin Gilbey and I do. 'Quinny' was the doyen of the press room when I first went racing, and he was in no doubt about what he had witnessed that day on October 3, 1965, at Longchamp. In his 40 years as a reporter, he had seen nothing to compare with it. In my 40 years as a reporter since then, neither have I.

Quinny knew it instantly, and filed a marvellous report for the following day's *Sporting Chronicle* to spread his knowledge. I was there on a busman's, so had no readers to tell. Anyway, nobody would have cared for the opinion of one who had such limited experience.

I was writing just for myself when I filled a few pages of a little blue notebook on the train back from Paris. Lest I should ever forget, I wanted to preserve my immediate thoughts on the magnificent spectacle I felt profoundly privileged to have seen. And I wound up those jottings wondering whether I would ever see such a sight again.

It was sunny and quite warm on that day in the Bois de Boulogne, but there had been plenty of rain in the preceding week and the ground was soft. Sea-Bird was a natural favourite after his Derby and Saint-Cloud triumphs, but he could hardly expect a pushover in that Arc.

We couldn't be sure that he was even France's best three-year-old, with unbeaten Jockey-Club, Grand Prix de Paris and Royal-Oak victor Reliance among his rivals. He also had to contend with the best of Ireland's (Meadow Court) and America's (Tom Rolfe) Classic crop, the two best English older horses (Oncidium and Soderini), Russia's all-time champion (Anilin), major recent winners in Germany (Demi Deuil) and Italy (Marco Visconti) and other prominent home team representatives such as Diatome, Free Ride, Carvin and Blabla – all Group 1 standard in today's terms.

Perched on a wall at the back of the old stand, I captured the denouement and finale of an epic performance – Marco Visconti and Anilin giving way, Sea-Bird and Reliance together in front, just momentarily, then one was gone, leaving the other for dead.

A field that had been bunched at the turn from home was suddenly spread out. At the finish it was six lengths back to Reliance, five more to Diatome, a short neck to Free Ride, half a length to Anilin, five to Tom Rolfe, six to Demi Deuil, and a length and a half to Carvin.

I couldn't know on October 3 just how good that was – even though Sea-Bird's lucky pilot Pat Glennon declared him the best horse he had ever seen, let alone ridden. It did not take long to find out, though. On October 17, Anilin won the Preis von Europa by four lengths. On November 4, Demi Deuil won the Premio Roma by seven. On November 11, Diatome and Carvin ran one-two in the Washington International, beating US Horse of the Year Roman Brother.

Then it was clear: no matter how long I spent in this game, I never would see anything to match the brilliance of that colt, nor the splendour of that occasion.

2 1971 2,000 Guineas Brigadier Gerard

The race was supposed to be a match between My Swallow and Mill Reef, the two best two-year-olds of 1970, separated by the minimum margin when they had clashed previously in France; each had been victorious in his comeback race, apparently confirming that they were still the leaders of the crop. Brigadier Gerard, without a previous run at three, cut them down and drew clear easily. It was the revelation of a superstar miler.

3 1965 Derby Sea-Bird

Sea-Bird, impressive in the Greffulhe and the Lupin, was a hot favourite because there were doubts about the quality of his rivals. In fact, runner-up Meadow Court promptly won the Irish Derby and the King George in impressive style. Sea-Bird had cantered over him all the way at Epsom in a display that suggested he was probably 14lb the better colt. We later learned that he was all of that.

4 1981 Derby Shergar

Shergar looked a class apart from his opposition on paper and duly proved the point, winning the 202nd edition of the premier Classic by the widest margin on record. The story goes that when John Matthias emerged from the pack on Glint Of Gold, he believed he was in front and had the race won. Shergar had flown, and he would have won by even further if Walter Swinburn had not eased him in the last 100 yards.

5 1975 King George Grundy

The Irish Guineas and dual Derby hero had to take on a crack four-year-old, Bustino, and the latter's two pacemakers, who were ridden to ensure that Grundy would never get a breather. He looked beaten on the home turn, but rallied to prevail after a pulsating duel. Dahlia, winner of the race in the two previous years, was a distant third, but even she beat the previous course record, which Grundy shattered by more than two seconds.

6 1970 King George Nijinsky

Nijinsky came to Ascot undefeated, with three Classics under his belt. He was naturally expected to win, but nobody imagined quite how he would do it, treating other Classic stars with total disdain. The worthy Blakeney was pressed into a full gallop without ever looking like mustering the pace that Nijinsky accomplished at a canter.

7 1968 Derby Sir Ivor

There were supposedly doubts about Sir Ivor's stamina for a mile and a half, and when stoutly bred Connaught still led, apparently full of running, into the last furlong, it seemed they were to be confirmed. An electrifying burst of acceleration dispelled that illusion in seconds.

8 1972 Derby Roberto

Of all Lester's great triumphs at Epsom, this was the finest – and the least appreciated. The crowd would presumably rather have seen Roberto finish second under Bill Williamson, but only Lester's brute strength could have got him home that day.

9 1967 King George Busted

Why does nobody else remember this exceptional performance? Busted had not shown much in Ireland as a three-year-old, but on his transfer to England – as the intended lead horse for Classic contender Royal Palace – he soon revealed unsuspected talent, at a higher level, indeed, than Royal Palace ever achieved. His thrashing of Salvo and Ribocco made a huge impression on me, and he would have won the Arc if he had not gone wrong.

10 1989 2,000 Guineas Nashwan

That majestic bearing in the paddock and that glorious flowing action in his canter to the start promised something special. And the gentle giant delivered just that on the way back up the Rowley Mile. He was sheer class that day, and went on to confirm his merit over ten furlongs and a mile and a half as well.

john randall's top ten

Racing's foremost historian **John Randall** with his view of the sport's greatest races

"About the best thing in racing is when two good horses single themselves out from the rest of the field and have a long-drawn-out struggle." So wrote George Lambton in his memoirs *Men And Horses I Have Known* about the battle between Ard Patrick and Sceptre in the 1903 Eclipse.

But a great race need not be in the balance until close home. It can involve a clash between two great horses with the champion of champions emerging victorious decisively, as happened in the 1851 match at York, the 1886 2,000 Guineas, the 1964 Cheltenham Gold Cup, and the 1971 2,000 Guineas; or it can throw up a performance of dazzling brilliance by a supreme champion crushing a top-quality international field.

However, there are other criteria for greatness in a race, including an awesome display of jumping, a magnificent weight-carrying performance, a sublime feat of training or jockeyship, a historic achievement, a fairytale farewell or comeback, a battling victory by a public favourite, and a last-gasp royal triumph.

None of the above criteria were satisfied by the 1913 Derby, but for drama, sensation, tragedy, controversy and intrigue, there has never been another race like it.

Emily Davison, a militant suffragette, ran out onto the course at Tattenham Corner and brought down the King's horse, Anmer. Aboyeur, a 100-1 no-hoper, led for most of the way, and after Craganour, the 6-4 favourite, joined him on the outside early in the straight, the pair literally battled it out to the line. Craganour's jockey forced Aboyeur onto the rail in order to block a challenger there, and as the struggle grew even more desperate, Aboyeur veered to the right, taking Craganour

wide and hampering challengers on the outside. Craganour eventually beat Aboyeur by a head. The first seven horses were separated by little more than a length, with others close behind.

The two principals looked equally guilty in a very rough race, but the stewards objected to Craganour and it was a sensation when they disqualified him. Eustace Loder, the presiding steward and breeder of Craganour, had a personal grudge against the colt's owner, Bower Ismay, and acted as prosecutor, judge and jury. Craganour thus became the only horse to be first past the post in both the 2,000 Guineas and the Derby without winning either. Charles Robinson, the judge, had mistakenly ruled Craganour to be only second in the Guineas, and in the Derby he failed to spot Day Comet, who finished third.

No other race has ever contained so many sensational and controversial incidents. Nowadays it would be analysed in slow motion from every conceivable angle, but in 1913 there were no technical aids, so there was only one opportunity to view it.

Given the chance to borrow one recording from a celestial video library of every race ever run, this is the one I would choose. Exactly what happened? Did Emily Davison deliberately target Anmer, was Aboyeur really more sinned against than sinning, and what was the exact finishing order? We can never be sure, and the 1913 Derby remains the most fascinating and elusive of races.

1 1913 Derby **2** 1973 Grand National **3** 1977 Templegate Hurdle **4** 1886 2,000 Guineas **5** 1962 Grand Steeple-Chase de Paris **6** 1903 Eclipse **7** 1965 Arc de Triomphe **8** 1964 Cheltenham Gold Cup **9** 1956 Arc de Triomphe **10** 1851 Match

the greatest races of 2005

If the poll had been later, how would the list have changed?

THERE is a school of thought that says the greatest race of all is the next one on the card. This book was handed a more definite remit, but one that was constrained by the march of time.

There were no races staged in 2005 that were eligible for the vote, but if the poll had been taken a year later there would have been plenty of candidates for inclusion on the grounds of freshness of recollection, if not absolute merit.

The Cheltenham Festival, always a fertile source of greatness, would certainly have provided a few prompts for voters. The incredible finish to Hardy Eustace's Champion Hurdle would probably have ensured its inclusion in the top 100, while Moscow Flyer's regaining of his Champion Chase crown would have drawn plenty of support through emotion alone.

Virtually every Derby attracts votes, but Motivator's triumphal progress might even have seen him take a top-50 position. Azamour's King George was a *tour de force* from horse and jockey, while the Juddmonte International saw five horses from (almost) the four corners of the world flatten out and fight for the prize through the final furlong – an exhilarating rarity at the highest level.

We had room for six; nothing from Royal Ascot at York appealed and the remaining Classics were short on the 'x-factor' necessary to propel them into the reckoning. So we thought a jump race would appeal to voters most, and the classic duel between Joes Edge and Cornish Rebel in the Scottish Grand National won our vote. Would it have won yours?

Edward Whitaker

Harchibald (centre) is still on the bridle, while Brave Inca (left) and Hardy Eustace are hard at work

Hardy Eustace and Harchibald

Champion Hurdle, Cheltenham, March 15, 2005

1 Hardy Eustace 7-2jf
2 Harchibald 7-1
3 Brave Inca 10-1

Winning owner Laurence Byrne
Trainer Dessie Hughes
Jockey Conor O'Dwyer
Distances nk, nk

What made it great An astounding denouement that left us gaping in amazement. The history books record that the courageous Hardy Eustace recorded his second successive Champion Hurdle victory at the head of an Irish whitewash, the visitors providing the first five home. However, most eyes were on the runner-up Harchibald, aboard whom Paul Carberry, exuding confidence, sat motionless until well after the final flight between Hardy Eustace and Brave Inca, both seemingly all out. Harchibald looked sure to be a clear-cut winner as soon as his rider said the word go – but his rider did not do so until 50 yards from the line, by which time Hardy Eustace had pulled out a fraction more, enough to hold off his rival. **NG**

Action Images

Moscow Flyer raises the roof

Queen Mother Champion Chase, Cheltenham, March 16, 2005

1 Moscow Flyer 6-4f
2 Well Chief 7-2
3 Azertyuiop 2-1

Winning owner Brian Kearney **Trainer** Jessica Harrington **Jockey** Barry Geraghty **Distances** 2l, 13l

What made it great Moscow Flyer, an outstanding horse, amply demonstrated his superiority with a consummate display that took his record over fences at the time to 18 wins from 18 completed chases. Although the race was billed as a clash between three gifted two-milers, only one of them mattered in the end as Moscow Flyer regained his crown, clearly only loaned out to Azertyuiop in 2004 when the Irish star had unseated his rider at Cheltenham. This time Azertyuiop made the telling error, losing all chance midrace and thereby robbing the contest of some of its intrigue, and Moscow Flyer never looked in any danger from Well Chief, a top-class horse in his own right. A victory both convincing and popular, it was greeted with a raucous reception from the crowd. **NG**

Moscow Flyer has the measure of Well Chief at the final fence

Walsh is edged out

Scottish Grand National, Ayr, April 16, 2005

1 Joes Edge 20-1
2 Cornish Rebel 9-2
3 Another Rum 10-1

Winning owner Chemipetro Ltd **Trainer** Ferdy Murphy **Jockey** Keith Mercer **Distances** sh hd, 10l

What made it great Ruby Walsh was eyeing a National clean sweep following his wins in Wales (Silver Birch), Ireland (Numbersixvalverde) and England (Hedgehunter), and when he sent Cornish Rebel past Joes Edge after the last the Grand Slam looked in his grasp. But that was reckoning without the will to win of Joes Edge and Keith Mercer, who valiantly refused to concede defeat that easily and rallied again on the rail. Despite Walsh's efforts Cornish Rebel seemed to be idling in front, and that was the spur Joes Edge needed. Fifty yards out he pulled level, and in a head-bobbing finish after four miles and a furlong he poked his nose back in front on the line, robbing Walsh of a place in the record books by a finger-width. **SD**

Cornish Rebel (left) and Joes Edge are locked in combat on the run-in

Ian Stewart pictures

AFP

Majestic Motivator

Derby, Epsom, June 4, 2005
1 Motivator 3-1f
2 Walk In The Park 11-1
3 Dubawi 5-1

Winning owner Royal Ascot Racing Club **Trainer** Michael Bell **Jockey** Johnny Murtagh **Distances** 5l, 3l

What made it great The magnificent manner of victory by a horse who had been at the forefront of Derby conjecture throughout the winter. Victory in the Racing Post Trophy as a juvenile had given him Derby credentials and his trainer delivered him to Epsom in the peak of condition following a prep win in the Dante. Murtagh rode a copybook Derby race, following the front two round Tattenham Corner and then kicking for glory halfway up the straight. Two furlongs out Motivator had all his rivals on the stretch, and he came away in the manner of a Generous, a Nashwan, a Troy to stamp his presence on the season. His 230 owners were not the only ones to leave the racecourse with a sense of wonder. **SD**

Motivator has nothing to fear from the fast-finishing Walk In The Park (second left)

Azamour stays the course

King George, Newbury, July 23, 2005

1 Azamour 5-2f

2 Norse Dancer 50-1

3 Bago 5-1

Winning owner HH the Aga Khan **Trainer** John Oxx **Jockey** Mick Kinane **Distances** 1¼l, sh hd

What made it great Would he stay? Azamour had Group 1 credentials at a mile and a mile and a quarter, and was trying a mile and a half for the first time in the toughest company imaginable. Only Oaks winner Eswarah represented Classic form, but the older brigade included Arc winner Bago, the previous year's winner Doyen, Irish Derby hero Grey Swallow and the tough duo Warrsan and Phoenix Reach. Kinane settled Azamour in at the back until squeezing open the throttle with three furlongs to run and swooped to take it up from Bago at the distance. If his stamina were to fail him it would be now ... but he strode on strongly to land the spoils with something up his sleeve. **SD**

Mick Kinane drives Azamour clear of Norse Dancer (right) and Bago

Press Association / David Davies

Top of the world

Juddmonte International, York, August 16, 2005

1 Electrocutionist 9-2
2 Zenno Rob Roy 4-1
3 Maraahel 8-1

Winning owner Earle Mack
Trainer Valfredo Valiani in Italy
Jockey Mick Kinane
Distances nk, hd

What made it great For once, the great York contest lived up to its name, with leading contenders from Britain, Ireland, Japan and Italy – although on balance it was by no means the classiest renewal of the race.

The Irish horse Ace made the running, with Zenno Rob Roy from Japan and Electrocutionist from Italy in arrears in a field of seven. Two furlongs out the picture changed, as Zenno Rob Roy, Maraahel and Norse Dancer came to challenge, and a furlong out there were five stretched across the track as Kinane brought Electrocutionist down the stands' side to join issue. Maraahel looked to hold the call, then Zenno Rob Roy, under an unremarkable Yutaka Take ride, took over, but Kinane and Electrocutionist were by now in full cry and snatched the spoils in the last three strides. **SD**

From left: Electrocutionist, Zenno Rob Roy, Ace, Maraahel and Norse Dancer go line abreast through the final furlong

Edward Whitaker

the greatest race I ever saw
1992 Sussex Stakes

by Ian Balding

IN 1992 we had in the yard a horse, Selkirk, who had been the top miler in Europe the previous season as a three-year-old, when he had won the Queen Elizabeth II Stakes at Ascot in most impressive style.

That Group 1 victory had only been made possible by a remarkable operation by our vet, Simon Knapp, who had removed under local anaesthetic one of the horse's testicles that was trapped in the inguinal canal and causing him discomfort. After the operation he was a totally different horse and went from strength to strength, and was later to become one of the most fertile and successful stallions in Europe.

Selkirk matured considerably over the winter and, when he won his first start as a four-year-old, the Lockinge Stakes at Newbury, I thought he might go on to prove himself one of the best milers of the decade. However, the unpredictability of racing was shown again when he ran a lacklustre race, finishing out of the money for the only time in his career, in the Prix d'Ispahan at Longchamp. He came back from France coughing and we had no option but to miss Royal Ascot and wait for the Sussex Stakes at Goodwood.

After a good rest, Selkirk was working beautifully in the build-up but was slightly inconvenienced by a bang on his joint and had to miss one work morning. But he still arrived at Goodwood in what I felt was peak form. Marling was a brilliant three-year-old filly, by Lomond out of the superb sprinter Marwell, trained by Geoff Wragg. She was unbeaten as a two-year-old, winning the Cheveley Park, and though unluckily beaten by Hatoof in the 1,000 Guineas, she had gone on to win both the Irish 1,000 and the Coronation Stakes at Royal Ascot.

Thus the stage was set for a great match between the outstanding four-year-old colt and the best three-year-old filly at their perfect distance of a mile. The remainder were also a talented bunch in their own right, including the previous year's Sussex Stakes winner Second Set, Breeders' Cup Sprint winner Sheikh Albadou, and three other highly rated milers in Sikeston, Rudimentary and Star Of Cozzene. Thourios made up the field of eight.

Marling started as 11-10 favourite with Selkirk at 7-2. Thourios set a furious pace followed by habitual front-runner Rudimentary, perhaps trying to test Marling and Sheikh Albadou's suspect stamina. Marling, ridden by Pat Eddery, settled in third place, about five lengths behind, with Ray Cochrane on Selkirk stalking her a few lengths further back.

With about a furlong and a half to run Pat got to the leaders and took over. Almost at once, Selkirk joined the filly and I felt that Ray had timed his late run to perfection. The big horse hit the front with 100 yards to run and I thought he would win, but the filly got back up to deny him by a head on the nod.

It was an exhilarating race between two outstanding milers, and although our horse was defeated, it remains firmly in my memory as one of the finest races I ever watched. It may even have been the finest.

Goodwood, July 29, 1992: **1** Marling (P Eddery) 11-10f
2 Selkirk 7-2 **3** Second Set 7-2. Trainer: G Wragg

the greatest race I ever saw
1987 Red Spinner Graduation
by Richard Birch

THE epic duel between Steve Cauthen and Pat Eddery for the 1987 Flat jockeys' title encapsulated all that is great about racing. From March to November, from Brighton to Edinburgh, these two champions fought a relentless, roller-coaster battle. It was American style and natural brilliance versus Irish power and never-say-die determination.

In those teenage student days, the concept of value didn't occupy my thoughts as a punter. Prices didn't matter; I just wanted winners. Fortunately, I was obsessed with the Henry Cecil stable – and it was a good year for such an obsession. 'HRA' enjoyed his greatest campaign with Reference Point, Indian Skimmer, Diminuendo, Paean and Orban gracing the Turf. He saddled seven winners at Royal Ascot; I backed six of them.

As Windsor's last evening meeting of the summer dawned, my pockets were bulging from the proceeds of Cecil's exceptional talent. Thirty pounds was my normal stake, but greed, cockiness, and a self-assurance that I couldn't lose overcame me that warm night.

Gesualdo was trained by Cecil, ridden by Cauthen and carried my 'lucky' black-and-white Charles St George colours. He was 11-10 favourite for the Red Spinner Graduation Stakes. Cecil seemed to win nearly all such races that year. Cauthen or Willie Ryan rode them. And I backed them.

Gesualdo was ground-breaking territory for me. From £30 punter to £100 punter in one step. Cauthen, the best judge of pace there's ever been, immediately took Gesualdo to the front. Race over. "£210, please, Mr Bookie." Oh, the impetuousness of youth.

"Come on Steve," I growled, as a two-length lead was halved at the three-furlong pole. My heart raced and the binoculars trembled. Kirpan and Eddery ranged upsides. The cockiness was gone. For the next two furlongs, Gesualdo and Kirpan were locked together stride for stride. Cauthen's beautifully streamlined aerodynamics versus Eddery's all-action, whackety-whack style.

Inside the final furlong, it appeared brute strength would win. Kirpan went a neck up. No panic from Cauthen. Galvanised into one final effort by those magical hands, Gesualdo rallied. Ten yards from the line the pair were once again inseparable. I was shaking like an old fairground generator as I contemplated the possibility of defeat. "Have you won, Steve?" A good-natured shrug, and a hint of a warm smile. How I loved him.

"Did you get it, Pat?" Blankety blank. Typical Pat. Refusal even to acknowledge my presence. How I longed for him to get beaten.

It was 20 minutes of torment before the verdict came. Yeeeeeessssss!

It was a landmark moment in this punter's career, and a crucial psychological blow for Eddery in his quest to be champion. Instead of beating Cauthen 3-1 on the night, he went home cursing a 2-2 draw.

There were still ten weeks of the season left, but I'm convinced that night – and that ride – is the one that determined the destination of the jockeys' title for 1987.

Cauthen won it by two, 197 to 195, which shows just how important Gesualdo was to a rider whose brilliance in the saddle that year remains unmatched.

Windsor, August 29, 1987: **1** Gesualdo (S Cauthen) 11-10f
2 Kirpan 5-1 **3** Johnny Rose 15-8. Trainer: H Cecil

the greatest race I ever saw
1968 Commander III Cup
by Michael Clower

WHEN I reached the racecourse I was told that the senior steward wanted to see me. The ex-army major, still with military moustache, told me that the stewards had considered my request to ride against the professionals at Nairobi the following week but felt I hadn't enough experience. I'd only ridden in one race.

This was an unexpected setback. I had already bought a horse to ride in the big time and, with the brashness of youth, replied: "Don't make your mind up yet. I'm riding this afternoon. Watch how I get on and, if you still don't think I'm up to it, then fair enough."

I knew my mount Fleet was a certainty in the Commander III Cup, a race confined to European amateurs and African professionals. She would have won the previous time if I hadn't given her too much to do in the short straight. I'd also lost two lengths at the start, where the mickey-takers said I was busy taking notes for my report in the *East African Standard*, the paper for which I acted as part-time racing correspondent alongside my 'day' job as an accountant, the position that had taken me to Kenya in the first place in March 1967.

Fleet's trainer had a nervous tic in his left cheek, and this really became apparent when he put the money down. I was glad to see it working overtime as he legged me into the saddle, saying: "If you go on going down the clubhouse hill, they'll never catch you."

Limuru is a tight, hilly circuit like Tramore, only the other way round. The starter, another ex-military man, called the roll. In Kenya old soldiers never died, they got a job with the Jockey Club instead.

This time I was off on terms and settled Fleet on the rail a few lengths behind the leaders. I concentrated on keeping her settled and going the shortest way round. Passing the clubhouse, I shot her through a narrow gap and we were clear. Turning into the straight, I showed her the whip and she lengthened her stride. For good measure I gave her a crack. The ears went back and I heard the tail swish, but she kept up the gallop.

While this might not, to take the phrase literally, have been the greatest race I ever saw, it certainly qualifies as *my* greatest race. After such a prestigious victory, I simply touched my cap to acknowledge the applause as I rode into the winner's enclosure, trying not to grin. If Lester Piggott showed no emotion even when he won the Derby, I shouldn't either!

Returning to weigh in, I passed one of the jockeys I now knew I would be riding against the following Sunday. "You prick," he said. "What did you hit her for?"

Seven days of starvation and dehydration later I was down to 7st 11lb. I sat in the jockeys' room feeling cold, nervous and dying of thirst. Not a drop of liquid had passed my lips for 48 hours.

The senior steward came into the room and walked over, I assumed to wish me luck. "I don't give a damn whether you win or lose," he said. "Just keep out of the way of the professionals. If I had my way, you wouldn't be riding here at all!"

Limuru, February 25, 1968: **1** Fleet (Mr M Clower) 4-1
2 Cornflakes 5-2 **3** Carronade 6-4f. Trainer: J Sprague

the greatest race I ever saw
1977 Champion Hurdle
by Graham Dench

WAS there ever a classier jump race than the 1977 Champion Hurdle? I doubt it.

While it is entirely understandable that the unforgettable dead-heat between Night Nurse and Monksfield in the Templegate Hurdle at Aintree was a popular choice among *Racing Post* readers, that race was effectively a match in which nothing else could be seriously fancied.

The Champion Hurdle, run just 17 days earlier, attracted a vastly superior field and produced a cracking finish, so it's something of a travesty that it didn't make the top 100.

On a personal level, I was a die-hard fan of the previous year's runner-up Birds Nest – blind to the claims of others and convinced his time had come. I'd been with him through thick and thin – mostly thick at that stage, although I still wince at the memory of his being brought down at the second under just 10st 7lb in the 1975 Schweppes – and he was a red-hot favourite, his wins that season including a breathtaking 15-length defeat of Night Nurse in the Fighting Fifth.

Master Monday, who had beaten Comedy Of Errors in the Sweeps Hurdle, was next in the betting, followed by Dramatist, who had beaten both Night Nurse and Birds Nest in the Christmas Hurdle.

The reigning champion Night Nurse, his crown seemingly having slipped a little and the heavy going a major worry, was only fourth best, while Sea Pigeon and Monksfield, hard though it is to credit with the benefit of hindsight, traded at double-figure odds.

Paddy Broderick sent Night Nurse straight out into the lead, as usual, and the gelding's jumping was as fast and fluent as ever. Although headed at the third-last by Birds Nest's stablemate Beacon Light, the previous year's Supreme Novices' winner, he was back in front two out and looking set to assert.

Dramatist and Monksfield were both closing, however, and so too was Night Nurse's stable-companion Sea Pigeon, who had been kept wide under a patient ride. Approaching the last an epic battle was in prospect, with Monksfield and Dramatist both more or less upsides, and Sea Pigeon poised for a late burst.

Crucially, Night Nurse got the best jump, and with the stiff uphill finish playing to his strengths, he would not be passed. Monksfield battled up the hill gallantly for a two-length second, putting up a performance that might have won him nine out of ten Champion Hurdles. Dramatist gave his all but was a similar distance back in third, then came Sea Pigeon, whose speed was blunted by the conditions.

And Birds Nest? To my horror, when the whip came out approaching the second-last, he hung left and faded into fifth.

I left the course struggling to fathom how my hero had been beaten so comprehensively.

Little did I know that a golden age of hurdling had dawned, and this would become the Champion Hurdle against which all others must be measured. Monksfield won the next two Champions; Sea Pigeon the two after that.

Birds Nest couldn't win the Champion in six attempts. It's not really any wonder he struggled that day.

Cheltenham, March 16, 1977: **1** Night Nurse (P Broderick) 15-2 **2** Monksfield 15-1 **3** Dramatist 6-1. Trainer: M H Easterby

the greatest race I ever saw
2000 Ascot Stakes
by Sir Clement Freud

I COULD undoubtedly bore people for a very long time on this particular subject.

Last Suspect's Grand National victory, with Hywel Davies bringing the horse from nowhere to enter the history books, was truly memorable. What about Lester Piggott's amazing Breeders' Cup win on Royal Academy by a neck, and the courage of the commentator who called the result although the two contestants raced on opposite sides of the track? Shergar's Derby? Dawn Run's Cheltenham Gold Cup? None of these will do for me. The 5.30 on the Wednesday of Royal Ascot 2000 takes pride of place.

In Las Vegas I once came across a dotty old lady playing the one-armed bandits wearing a single shoe with her hair in curlers. When I gave her a question-mark look, she explained that when some years ago she had won a $100,000 jackpot on these very machines, she'd kicked off one shoe and had just been to a neighbourhood hair salon.

For similar reasons, the Wednesday of Royal Ascot has become the day I take an extra thick wad of notes to the track.

The Ascot Stakes is a two-and-a-half-mile handicap that rates low on the totem pole of distance races, with the winner more likely to follow up in a hurdle at Newton Abbot than a prestigious test at Goodwood or York.

I seldom stay for final races because of my resentment at all the queues, the ones for getting out of racecourse car parks coming top of my list. But in 2000, the 5.30 at Royal Ascot, which did not get away until 5.40, was different. I had backed Observatory at 8-1 in the first race; Romantic Myth, the 4-1 favourite in the second; and Caribbean Monarch in the Hunt Cup.

And because I had had a goodish Tuesday, I put those three into a Lucky 15 with Barba Papa in the last. My friend Marten Julian had tipped me Barba Papa, trained by AJ Martin, ridden by JP Murtagh, joint-third favourite at 10-1. So it came to pass that with three winners in my bet, I spent the hour prior to the Ascot Stakes filling sheets of paper to determine the result of the Irish horse winning. The sum was in excess of £70,000.

After that, I would have to queue to get out of the car park, although I presumed I would be among the happier punters in that queue. Barba Papa won by a length and a bit; I watched from my box and as he passed the post, I galloped to the exit to hear, just as I got to the main gates, the words "stewards' inquiry, hold your tickets".

I could have waited, but felt that my presence on the course would make no difference to the outcome of deliberations by the men in bowler hats, and left. Turned on the car radio; nothing from Ascot. Did not then have a mobile phone, so drove home determined to stop at a bookmaker's in Hammersmith to glean the result. Could not park in Hammersmith, drove down Shepherds Bush road and tried William Hill's. It was closed. Got home, was going to turn on the television and then thought: "Hell, it seems greedy to race to the television set," and made myself a quiet cup of tea.

Then I learnt the result: Barba Papa.

I xeroxed the cheque before I sent it to my bank.

Royal Ascot, June 21, 2000: **1** Barba Papa (J P Murtagh) 10-1
2 Seliana 25-1 **3** Heros Fatal 9-4f. Trainer: A J Martin

the greatest race I ever saw
1986 Arc de Triomphe
by Paul Haigh

FOR a long time, I thought the best race I'd ever seen was a handicap hurdle at Sandown in 1970 that Bula won by a short head. It can't have been a bad one, as the great hurdler passed no fewer than 12 others on the run-in, and was carrying 12st 1lb when he did it. I got so tensed up by the sight of it that my spine locked for about ten minutes after it was over – a strange and unpleasant sensation, and one that fills you with great joy when it goes away.

Then I realised that a large component in the thrill of that race was the fact that Bula was the last leg of a 20p Yankee – a substantial investment in those days, and one that guaranteed I'd be able to buy my round for several days. Maybe even weeks.

So the memory may have been, in fact almost certainly was, corrupted by vile pecuniary interest. Besides, you can't have a hurdle race as your greatest ever, can you? Not when you've finally reached the conclusion that Flat racing is the sport you truly love.

I therefore have to go for the greatest Flat race I've ever seen. Or rather for the greatest Flat race I didn't actually see live – and which, thanks to the way the race panned out, and the vandalistic incompetence of a French TV cameraman, perhaps hardly anyone who wasn't at the front of the upper tiers of the Longchamp stands on the first Sunday in October 1986 ever saw properly. (Although no doubt, as with Gareth Edwards' try, Gordon Banks's save from Pele, the Botham-Willis Test match and the Rumble in the Jungle, all sorts of people who were nowhere near the places where these epic events unfolded will swear blind they were witnesses to every step, every moment, every punch.)

I wasn't there for Dancing Brave's Arc. For some reason I went to Øvrevoll on that memorable Sunday to watch Acarine in the Norwegian Grand National.

You did what? I hear you cry. Well yes, I did. Partly because I'd been to Arcs before. Partly because I thought Dancing Brave would probably get beaten by a stronger stayer. Partly because, to be completely honest, I was still a fully paid-up member of the Scandinavian Fantasists' League at the time, and felt reasonably confident I was going to be met at Oslo airport by gangs of Agnetha-from-Abba lookalikes, in starched white nurse's uniforms, with magnums of Aquavit under one arm and jeroboams of baby oil under the other.

It wasn't quite like that – although not so completely different as you might think – but even though Acarine won, and even though the party afterwards was excellent in every respect, I've never regretted a trip so much.

To have been there in Paris to see the burst that took that brilliant horse past eight Group 1 winners in half a furlong; to have the sight of it burned in my brain; to have been able to say, truthfully, "I was there"; most of all not to have had to spend so much time since cursing the poor Frog who 'lost' him as he careered down the outside with a run that reduced the normally phlegmatic Pat Eddery to something close to tears in the post-race interview – I'd have given up almost anything for that. Maybe even the chance to meet Agnetha-from-Abba herself.

Longchamp, October 5, 1986: **1** Dancing Brave (P Eddery) 11-10f
2 Bering 11-4 **3** Triptych 64-1. Trainer: G Harwood

the greatest race I ever saw
1994 2,000 Guineas
by Mark Johnston

WHAT makes a race great? Is it the quality of the competitors, the excitement it generates, or the emotion that it raises?

While I firmly believe that the quality of the competitors is crucial – it is virtually impossible to call anything from a second or third division 'great' – I am not one for comparing the merits of individual horses, or any athletes, from different generations.

Where there are no direct lines of form, comparisons are reduced to little more than subjective opinion. It seems that most of those who attempt to put arithmetical values on horses' ability choose to ignore all scientific measurements such as time, actual distance travelled or wind speed, and prefer to base their evaluations on the style, or manner, of the victory and the distances between competitors at the finish. To my mind their methods are useless when applied to horses who had no opportunity to meet.

It has been said that I could start an argument in an empty house, and I certainly express my opinions forcibly but, when push comes to shove, the scientist in me will usually prevent me from claiming opinions as fact.

If pushed to pick a race with which I had no personal involvement, I'd go for the 1997 Nunthorpe. A dead-heat! The first woman jockey to win a Group 1 race! Kevin Darley riding without a bridle! And, to cap it all, Kieren Fallon like a circus rider trying to pull up Kevin's horse as they disappeared across the Knavesmire! If you wrote it as a film script it would be rejected as too fanciful.

However, I could not base my choice of greatest race simply on my estimation of merit or ability; I had to look at the effect that race had on me personally and those closest to me. With this in mind, I was immediately drawn to the performances of Double Trigger. Every race he ran, from the record-breaking maiden at Redcar to his swansong in the Doncaster Cup, had a story to go with it. Memories of the crowds running to the winner's enclosure at Goodwood when he won his third Goodwood Cup, or when he outbattled his brother, Double Eclipse, to take that race for the first time in 1995, almost had my mind made up for me.

But I couldn't put pen to paper without having one last look at Mister Baileys winning the 2,000 Guineas in 1994. I have more memories of that day than of any other in my racing career. I remember exactly where I stood to watch the race, the people around me, my feelings and reactions as he hit the front and stayed there to the line, and the first person I spoke to as I rushed down out of the stands. I remember the feeling of panic when he didn't appear with the other horses coming off the track, and the relief and pride when I realised he was being held back for a grand welcome to the winner's enclosure. I didn't, however, remember it all: a review of the video showed me just how ecstatic the owner and all the other connections were. The groom and the other attendants made no attempt to hide their excitement; crowd and media joined in.

It was the reaction of the people that made it a great race, a great day and, ultimately, a great year for me. It was, without doubt, the greatest race I ever saw.

Newmarket, April 30, 1994: **1** Mister Baileys (J Weaver) 16-1 **2** Grand Lodge 16-1 **3** Colonel Collins 13-2. Trainer: M Johnston

the greatest race I ever saw
1969 Coronation Cup
by Marten Julian

IT makes such a difference when you are there.

It makes even more of a difference when you are there as a star-struck teenager. In those days it was a treat to be picked up from boarding school for a day out, whatever the reason.

That day in June 1969 was very special. A friend's father had promised to take us out for a day at Epsom races.

When I sneaked off to the local betting shop during many a school lunch break, the horses and jockeys were no more than chalked-up names on a blackboard.

Of course, we knew that Lester Piggott was someone special, but we didn't know that jockeys' silks shimmered in the sun or that horses made rude noises when they galloped to post.

In those days the Downs were packed with people and buses for the Derby meeting, even on the supporting days. I had never seen anything like it in my life.

The highlight of the day was the Coronation Cup, a race worth £11,457 6s to the winner. The 9-4 favourite was Remand, with Park Top second best at 11-4. The mighty Connaught was also in the field while there, in the flesh, were the top riders of their time – Lewis, Hutchinson, Barclay, Mercer and Lindley.

It was when the horses passed the stands, before returning to make their way back across the Downs to the Derby start, that I fell under the spell that was to change the course of my life.

I had never ridden a horse and had certainly never seen a live sporting event of any note. But something about the way the mare and her rider went down to post drew me in. So, indeed, did the bookmakers, to the tune of five shillings – a significant proportion of the £2 pocket money that was expected to provide for me through the long summer term.

Spellbound, I watched as the preliminaries unfolded before me. Following a lengthy delay, caused by the antics of Ribero, the stalls opened and the race was off.

Hipster made the running for the first half-mile or so before Connaught adopted his customary role at the head of proceedings, with Piggott and Park Top biding their time.

With three furlongs to go Connaught was still galloping strongly while Piggott, to my astonishment and horror, was sitting motionless. Mount Athos then came to challenge on the outside, but still Piggott refused to move.

Then, about 100 yards from the line, Piggott allowed the mare her head. Guided through the gap between her two rivals she eased to the front, only for Piggott to then drop his hands. Park Top passed the post three-quarters of a length ahead of Mount Athos.

Such disdain. Such confidence. Such arrogance. All the qualities I, a gawky 16-year-old, so lacked.

So why, then, does the 1969 Coronation Cup qualify as my favourite race? The answer is simple.

It's because I saw, for the first time, that special bond that can exist between a man and a horse. It's a race I have never forgotten.

And I never will.

Epsom, June 5, 1969: **1** Park Top (L Piggott) 11-4
2 Mount Athos 100-7 **3** Connaught 11-4. Trainer: B van Cutsem

the greatest race I ever saw
1984 Doncaster Stakes
by Bill O'Gorman

THE most exciting race of your life need not be an important event in the overall scheme of things. It may well owe its place among your memories to a personal satisfaction not necessarily appreciated by the rest of the world.

That's how I made my choice. By the time Provideo lined up for the Doncaster Stakes in late October, he had already won 14 of his 22 starts – including the Cock of the North Stakes at Haydock and the Champion 2-Y-O Trophy at Ripon – but we had set our hearts on at least equalling the record for the most victories by a two-year-old in Britain, which stood at 16, achieved by The Bard in 1885 (with the luxury of a walkover!)

Time was rapidly running out for Provideo after Doncaster, as there was just one more opportunity before the end of the season. Put simply, he had to win both races to match The Bard – and, at the four-day stage, it became obvious that, due to his penalties, this race was far from a foregone conclusion, particularly for a juvenile at the end of such a gruelling season.

Provideo, though, was Kiplingesque in his apparent ability to treat victory and defeat with equal disdain, and, even though he had been defeated in three of his previous four starts and although five furlongs was palpably no longer his optimum trip, we were obliged to run if there was to be any chance of his equalling the record.

The main danger clearly came from a horse called Pacific Gold, trained by Eric Eldin and ridden by Taffy Thomas. Although this horse had two or three seconds in useful company

and had recently run respectably in Group company at Ascot, he remained a maiden and thus received 15lb from Provideo under the conditions of the race. That was a sizeable pull; perhaps too much for us.

Ironically, this was a horse with whom I was perfectly familiar. He had been bred by Peter Nurse, who was a great friend of mine, and he had been previously ridden by Tony Ives, who always rode Provideo. We would have far rather not have had to cope with Pacific Gold on such unfavourable terms, but there was no alternative.

That a friend had bred Pacific Gold and our second jockey Taffy Thomas rode him added a little edge to the confrontation. However, that was as nothing compared to the fact that Pacific Gold was owned by one of my chief owners, Mrs Yong! As far as I can recall, this subject was never mentioned between us either before or after the event. Which is probably just as well.

Provideo set out to make all, despite the weight, because he needed further, but when Mrs Yong's gold-and-red diamonds – the colours that had been carried by so many winners from the O'Gorman stable in the past – appeared to get past his green-and-red blinkers just inside the last furlong, my feelings can probably be imagined.

Battling with his customary tenacity, however, Provideo got back up in the shadow of the post, where the sun, for once, was shining on the righteous! And there was a happy ending as far as we were concerned, as Provideo went on to record his 16th win in a minor event at Redcar in November.

Doncaster, October 26, 1984: **1** Provideo (T Ives) 2-1f
2 Pacific Gold 9-4 **3** Prismatic 9-4. Trainer: W O'Gorman

the greatest race I ever saw
1988 Breeders' Cup Distaff

by Rachel Pagones

THE best races are the ones in which you get personally involved. That can happen when your money is tied up in the result, but to me it always meant a lot more when my heart was tied up in the result, when one horse in the race caught my imagination so much I felt like it was me straining towards the wire.

That was never more so than in 1988, when Personal Ensign won the Breeders' Cup Distaff at Churchill Downs. She may have been regally bred and exquisitely well connected – a daughter of Private Account and Grecian Banner, she was part of the Ogden Mills Phipps dynasty and conditioned by his private trainer, Shug McGaughey – but she'd known adversity, having raced with five screws in one leg for most of her career.

That didn't stop her from winning all 12 of her races before the Breeders' Cup, though. She only got stronger as she grew older, and already as a four-year-old she'd added six Graded races to her score.

So Personal Ensign was headed into this race, which we all knew would be her last, with an unbeaten record to defend. If she did it, she would become the first top-rank American thoroughbred to retire undefeated since Colin in 1908.

That was one theme of this Breeders' Cup. Another revolved around the presence of Kentucky Derby winner Winning Colors in the race – the first time a Derby winner would be in the line-up of the Distaff.

And yet another: the magnificent Alysheba was taking a second stab at winning the Classic, after losing by a nose to Ferdinand in 1987. If he won, he would surely be Horse of the Year, but if he lost and Personal Ensign prevailed in the Distaff, well, the title could be hers.

On top of it all, she was ridden by my favourite jockey, Randy Romero, whose life seemed like one long hard-luck story.

I was living in northern Florida at the time, and a bunch of us gathered in someone's mobile home (everyone in Florida lived in a mobile home – the rich people had double-wides) to watch the races. Outside the windows were live oaks draped with Spanish moss, but I don't remember the weather; not in Florida, anyway.

At Churchill Downs in Kentucky it was a miserably cold, wet day, and by the time of the Distaff – the third race on the Breeders' Cup card – the track was officially muddy. For a filly who was wrapping up a full season, racing with hardware in her bones against a front-running Kentucky Derby winner, it looked like 13 could be the unlucky number.

And it continued to look that way, with Winning Colors enjoying an easy lead while Personal Ensign fell back, got caught in tight quarters and ate mud for more than a mile. But the very last half-furlong was as valiant a performance as I've ever seen. As Tom Durkin's typically dramatic stretch call went: "At the 16th pole it looked like Personal Ensign was facing her first defeat, but in those final 110 courageous yards, she certainly proved herself a champion this afternoon."

That she did. It was great, all right.

Churchill Downs, November 5, 1988: **1** Personal Ensign (R Romero) 1-2f
2 Winning Colors 3-1 **3** Goodbye Halo 9-2. Trainer: C McGaughey

my greatest race – professionally speaking

We talked to a selection of racing personalities to find out which races they consider the most memorable

Clare Balding
1992 Sussex Stakes (Marling)

I watched this race at Goodwood standing next to my father Ian, who trained Selkirk. It was a tremendous battle through the final furlong and my father thought Selkirk was beaten, but, being ever-optimistic, I was convinced he had won. As usual, I was wrong. It was a great race. I only wish it had been a dead-heat.

Jack Berry
1993 King George Stakes (Lochsong)

It was a foggy day at Goodwood and you could barely see a thing, but Paris House and Lochsong jumped out and went nip and tuck all the way. They came out of the fog together after having battled for five furlongs solid and I'd never seen a race like it. It was incredible. Lochsong beat Paris House by a head – that is the race I'd take in my box with me when I go.

Jim Bolger
1968 Derby (Sir Ivor)

That Derby made a big impression on me. The race was run on a Wednesday back then and I took a day's holiday from work to watch it – I've never worked Derby Day, but conscientiously I've always taken it as holiday! – and was extremely impressed with the horse, the trainer, Vincent O'Brien, and the jockey, Lester Piggott.

Clive Brittain
1985 Breeders' Cup Turf (Pebbles)

It was a tremendous run. She was drawn on the wide outside, a bad draw, and everything had to go right for her. It did – and she managed to come through to win. That was certainly one of Pat Eddery's finest moments in the saddle.

Willie Carson
1980 Queen Elizabeth II Stakes (Known Fact)

This was one of the most gigantic battles, between me on Known Fact and Kris. Known Fact had won the Guineas slightly by default – he was beaten by a better horse in Nureyev and the inquiry had nothing to do with me – but Kris was practically unbeatable. It took a good 'un to beat him and Known Fact was a good 'un. Everything went right for me.

the professionals' choice

Henry Cecil
1980 Ascot Gold Cup (Le Moss)

Rather sentimentally, I am going for a race in which I was involved. Le Moss was lame through April and box-rested, yet despite being without a race that season he still led all the way to hold off the challenge of another great stayer in Ardross – who won the next two Gold Cups – by three-quarters of a length.

Mick Channon
1975 King George (Grundy)

When you think of great races, Grundy versus Bustino is the first one that comes to mind. The 2,000 Guineas with Brigadier Gerard, Mill Reef and My Swallow was another great one and there have been a lot of good races since, but Grundy and Bustino really sticks in the mind.

Luca Cumani
1994 Breeders' Cup Mile (Barathea)

For me, it is difficult to decide between Barathea and Falbrav's win in the 2003 Queen Elizabeth II Stakes, but the fact that up until then English-trained horses hadn't been doing particularly well in the Breeders' Cup, and there was a lot of pressure on us, just gives it to Barathea. He had blotted his copybook when running a bad bend the year before, but this time all the preparation went fantastically well and Frankie Dettori gave him a superb ride. When he unleashed him, he burst clear to win going away and set a track record. It was one of the most exhilarating days of my life.

Frankie Dettori
2000 Dubai World Cup (Dubai Millennium)

Because he lived up to expectations, and even more, in what was a top-class race. He destroyed them in such a way that you have to go back to Secretariat for something similar. He beat his own track record, that he'd set three weeks earlier. He remains the best horse I've ever ridden.

Pat Eddery
1986 Arc (Dancing Brave)

There was so much pressure on the horse that day – he was up against so many Group 1 winners and went off favourite for the race. He put up a truly great performance, we challenged last of all and he came by them on the wide outside. It was a real exciting day, absolutely incredible.

Richard Dunwoody
1990 Breeders' Cup Mile (Royal Academy)

I wasn't riding that day and had taken my father racing at Chepstow. John Reid was supposed to be on board Royal Academy but was injured, so Lester got the call-up. It was brilliant to see him back in the saddle and teaming up again with Vincent O'Brien. Lester has been one of my all-time heroes since I was five or six, and to win a Breeders' Cup at the age of 54 was something special.

David Elsworth
1988 Grand National (Rhyme 'N' Reason)

He all but came down at Becher's first time round – suffering an injury that prevented his ever running again – but made up all the ground he lost and was in front three-quarters of a mile out. Durham Edition went by him at the second-last but, having 'lost' the race twice, he rallied gamely and regained the lead 100 yards from the line. It really was a tremendous performance, unbelievable.

John Francome
1984 Whitbread (Special Cargo)

It has to be this one: it was a truly amazing contest. In a big race, you very seldom have three horses all in a line like that, with Special Cargo beating Lettoch and his own stablemate Diamond Edge. Utterly incredible – and, of course, made all the more memorable as it was the Queen Mother's horse who won.

Barry Geraghty
1994 Champion Chase (Viking Flagship)

It was a serious race. It was a really top two-miler and we saw a really gutsy performance by both horse and rider. I think Adrian Maguire launched Viking Flagship from outside the wings at the last, and it was a real battle up the hill against Deep Sensation and Travado. Viking Flagship was the underdog beforehand and it was just the complete performance from both horse and rider.

Alex Greaves
1997 Nunthorpe (Coastal Bluff/Ya Malak)

I'd have to choose one of my own and it has to be this one. Kevin Darley's bridle had broken on Coastal Bluff and I dead-heated with him on Ya Malak. It was the first Group 1 winner I rode and the first time a woman rider had ever won a Group 1. Coastal Bluff was also trained by David Barron, who I used to be apprentice for, so it was quite a local story.

Nicky Henderson
2004 Victor Chandler Chase (Isio)

You could go back and back to other races if you wanted, but I thought that was one of the greats. It was an epic – a real good two-mile chase. I thought Isio was beaten but, while he may not have been the biggest, he has a heart of gold. I felt sorry for the second, Azertyuiop, who ran an amazing race giving away 19lb. There are great days and there are great races, and that was definitely a great race.

Richard Johnson
1995 Melling Chase (Viking Flagship)

While I appreciate that the vast majority of people select a race in which they had an involvement, my only link was I worked in the yard where the winner was trained. But this race left an indelible memory like no other. Three terrific chasers jumped the final fence locked together and gave their all. Adrian Maguire was at his brilliant best on the winner.

the professionals' choice

Lisa Jones
2003 Jockey Club Cup (Persian Punch)

The one I think is the greatest was the last race that Persian Punch won. He looked beaten but he still managed to come back up again in the last few strides and win. Absolutely everyone was cheering for him that day. It was such a spectacular race and it just showed you what a courageous horse he was. He was one of my all-time favourite horses to watch and I know a lot of people think the same way.

Gay Kelleway
1971 Champion Hurdle (Bula)

It's got to be when my dad won on Bula in the Champion Hurdle. I must have been seven and knew nothing about it at the time, but dad got it on video in black and white and it is unbelievable. Everyone said that he'd left it too late. It looked as if he had given Bula an impossible task, but he knew where the winning post was and got up easily in the end. Incredible acceleration.

Mick Kinane
1993 Melbourne Cup (Vintage Crop)

We made history that day – the first European raiders to win the Melbourne Cup. It was a great occasion and it was great to be a part of it. We all put a lot of hard work into it, Dermot Weld and the whole team, and it was a fantastic achievement to pull it off. I've won a lot of big races but that one has left the biggest impression on me.

Henrietta Knight
1975 King George (Grundy)

This may surprise you a little, but I have no hesitation in naming that race as the greatest, as it was simply unbelievable – I was lucky enough to be there and it was the most exciting race I've ever seen. Neither Grundy nor Bustino deserved to be beaten.

Adrian Maguire
1995 Melling Chase (Viking Flagship)

Viking Flagship was an out-and-out battler who always jumped superbly and I really think it was guts that won on the day, rather than sheer ability. It was a brilliant race for me personally, but a great spectacle too. To see three two-mile champions racing like that is quite special. It really was jump racing at its best.

Ginger McCain
1973 Grand National (Red Rum)

I'd be telling a lie if I didn't say it was Red Rum getting up to beat Crisp. Certainly, that was very, very special indeed. I don't want to be boastful in any way, shape or form, because I was personally involved, but that race has to be up there with the greatest of all time.

Tony McCoy
1998 Aintree Hurdle (Pridwell)

The race in which Pridwell beat Istabraq by a neck has got to be one of the best of all time. The ground was dreadful that day, almost bottomless, but it didn't bother Pridwell, who got up on the run-in to beat one of the all-time great hurdlers in his prime. That, to me, was the greatest.

John McCririck
1993 2,000 Guineas (Zafonic)

On that day, over a mile, Zafonic was unbeatable. He swept from last to first to beat horses of the calibre of Barathea in track record time. He was the epitome of what a racehorse should be in that race. I can't imagine that any horse, in any Guineas, even the likes of Tudor Minstrel, could have withstood the fantastic burst of speed Zafonic produced.

J P McManus
1986 Cheltenham Gold Cup (Dawn Run)

Dawn Run's victory will live forever in my memory. Having looked beaten after jumping the last, the mare showed tremendous courage and battling qualities to force her way past Wayward Lad to the front, very ably assisted by an inspired Jonjo O'Neill. It was an incredible performance.

Johnny Murtagh
2001 Irish Champion Stakes (Fantastic Light)

It was hyped up to be between the two big horses – Galileo had beaten Fantastic Light in the King George. They were neck and neck for the last furlong and Fantastic Light got up to win by a head. I have never heard anything like that cheer, and the reception for the horses was incredible. It was a fantastic race.

Paul Nicholls
1999 Cheltenham Gold Cup (See More Business)

It has to be this race, for obvious reasons. It was a lifetime's ambition for the owners and a lifetime's ambition for me. To get 'See More' to win the Gold Cup – well, it was amazing. He was a great horse to me and everyone connected with him; without him I probably wouldn't be where I am today.

David Nicholson
1995 Melling Chase (Viking Flagship)

It would have to be Viking Flagship, Martha's Son and Deep Sensation at Aintree, when they were all upsides at the last. Any one of the three could have won. I was stood opposite the winning post and I didn't even know who had got it – exhilarating. The wait for the decision, though – that felt like an age.

the professionals' choice

Lord Oaksey
1958 Hennessy (Taxidermist)

It was certainly the most exciting race I've been involved in, and I rode in quite a few aboard Taxidermist. 'Taxi' must have jumped the last in fifth place, but he made up about a dozen lengths on the Cheltenham hill and just got up to beat Kerstin, who came back to win the race the following year, by a short head. It was a pretty close call.

Vincent O'Brien
1986 Punchestown match (Dawn Run)

This event gave me particular pleasure, as I was able to lend a hand in arranging the match, the first for many years. Both horses had won at Cheltenham – Buck House won the Champion Chase and Dawn Run the Gold Cup – and the public interest was incredible. At level weights, the two jumped the last three fences upsides, and the reception given to the mare after her narrow victory was truly memorable, made all the more poignant in hindsight as both horses suffered untimely deaths shortly afterwards. We saw two great performances by horses and jockeys, Tony Mullins and Tommy Carmody.

Edward O'Grady
1969 Arc (Levmoss)

It was my first Arc and I actually backed Park Top. Bill Williamson, who later became a pal, rode the race of his life to beat her on Levmoss. There wasn't much international racing at that time and it was a wonderful day to be Irish in Paris. Sensational.

John Oxx
1990 Breeders' Cup Mile (Royal Academy)

That was a fairytale race. The triumphant return of Lester Piggott after five years away from the saddle was an unbelievable event all round. He had only been back riding for a couple of weeks! If you were to think of the greatest races ever, that one would be hard to beat. It was a great night on one of racing's biggest stages.

Martin Pipe
1997 Champion Hurdle (Make A Stand)

This is a very memorable race to me. Make A Stand went off in front and led them a merry dance. When I watched the race, I was sure he'd stop up the hill. I shouted 'he's beat, he's beat, he'll stop'. But he didn't. He left them for dead; the race was over with four to jump. He was a joy to watch and a joy to train – he was exceptional.

Jenny Pitman
1991 Cheltenham Gold Cup (Garrison Savannah)

Garrison Savannah had a difficult preparation due to a shoulder problem and we'd trouble keeping him sound. My son Mark had been beaten on Toby Tobias in a close finish the previous year, and, after the leader Celtic Shot made a mistake at the third-last, he was left in front sooner than we'd planned. At the last I could see The Fellow was closing, and he continued to close up the run-in. At the line they were level, but separated by the width of the course. I didn't know who'd won. My mind was a blank; I was on auto-pilot.

Richard Quinn
1998 Lonsdale Stakes (Persian Punch)

It was a real thrill to ride Persian Punch and this was a fantastic finish, with four horses in with a chance of winning 400 yards out. Celeric, who had won both the Yorkshire Cup and Ascot Gold Cup the year before, went on for Pat Eddery but then sort of idled, and old Persian Punch got him back on the line to win by a short head, with Maridpour a neck away in third.

Peter Scudamore
1982 Schweppes Gold Trophy (Donegal Prince)

John Francome was down to ride at 10st 8lb and, in order to satisfy the clerk of the scales, had weighed out without his saddle. He'd been pretty grumpy before the race, as he'd been offered two or three mounts and wasn't sure if he'd chosen the right one. But he was absolutely brilliant in the event itself, scrubbing Donegal Prince along all the way and coming out best in a three-way photo-finish. What made it especially memorable was that he, Steve Smith Eccles and I had agreed to share our prize-money if any of us won. When Francome admitted that in a newspaper article, we all got done by the stewards!

Jamie Spencer
1986 Cheltenham Gold Cup (Dawn Run)

Dawn Run was the first racehorse I really took to – I must have been five or six at the time she caught my imagination – and I've got great memories of her. She and Desert Orchid were my favourites, and the best day with Dawn Run was the Gold Cup; the worst, obviously, was at Auteuil when she was killed.

Walter Swinburn
1972 Derby (Roberto)

I'd have to go back to the duel between Roberto and Rheingold. I was in school and was given permission to come out and watch the race because my father was riding Manitoulin. However, it was Lester who made an everlasting impression with his storming finish. It was some race, hard to forget. It didn't spoil it that Manitoulin finished down the field!

Derek Thompson
1981 Grand National (Aldaniti)

Bob Champion's victory on Aldaniti has to be number one. Against all the odds he fought his way back from cancer, not just to ride again but to win the world's greatest steeplechase on a horse who a couple of years earlier the vets had said should be put down. No argument – the greatest race has to be the 1981 Grand National.

Dermot Weld
1993 Melbourne Cup (Vintage Crop)

I remember it as a great day for Ireland. Although everyone said it couldn't be done, to win a big race in the southern hemisphere, I was always quietly confident. It was the first year anyone had done it, and considering all the problems we faced it was some achievement. You have no idea of the pleasure it gave me.

the readers' choice **winning letters**

The Racing Post asked its readers to submit a short argument in support of their choice, with prizes for the best five after the hundreds of letters and emails had been considered. Here, we reproduce the winning five – and the paper's letters editor Martin Smethurst explains exactly how the choice was made

AS OUR readers chose the 100 Greatest Races, I had the fascinating task of sifting through considerably more than that number of letters enthusiastically endorsing the nominations.

It certainly made picking the best five, the senders of which each won a copy of *Racing Post Flat Horses of 2004*, a tricky task. So tricky, in fact, that I enlisted a little help from Jo Yarborough, the deputy letters editor.

There is no doubt the search stirred the emotions, and many readers clearly have those moments of magnificent victory and agonising defeat playing on an endless loop in their minds – and were more than happy to be given the chance to air them to a (much!) larger audience.

The five winning letters not only captured the crowning glory of the great moments described, but, vitally, conveyed to us all just what a thrill was felt on a personal level. A thrill that, to these racing devotees at least, is guaranteed to last a lifetime.

The winning offerings came from various parts of Britain and Ireland and covered a considerable timespan. But that is not why they were chosen. They were chosen because, in our opinion, they were the best.

MARTIN SMETHURST

When I knew 'The Brave' would get his revenge
The 1986 Prix de l'Arc de Triomphe – and an unforgettable trip to see Dancing Brave at home

EVEN NOW, nearly 20 years on, whenever I see 'The Brave' swooping late on the outside to just get up in the 1986 Arc, I get goose pimples all over my body. Is it the fact that he beat the best Arc field ever assembled? Is it down to Eddery's perfect timing? Or is it more justification for that Derby defeat? No. It's all three!

As a young man of 23 and interested in racing, I wrote to Guy Harwood in the spring of 1986 and asked him if I could visit his stable. I was totally amazed when the great man replied (admittedly via his secretary) and said: "No problem."

I was given a date – the Friday before the Eclipse at Sandown – and told to be there by 7am. As I was driving down from Wales, I had to set off at 3.30am. I arrived at Coombelands just before seven and was greeted by Owen, head groom at the time. We went up to the gallops and watched three or four strings working before returning to the yard for breakfast at about nine. ·

It was then time for my tour of the barns to 'meet' the horses in their boxes. Halfway down the second barn I saw the name Dancing Brave untidily written in chalk on a blackboard on the gate.

Owen introduced him as the unlucky Derby runner-up but said he was a certainty for tomorrow's Eclipse. Even though he said he shouldn't, Owen then opened the door to the box and asked me if I wanted to go in. I murmured "yes" and took a few paces to be next to the flank of this great beast. As I patted him on the neck he turned his head to the side and began nodding. I still think he was saying to me: "Yes I know, I'll beat him next time."

As we all know, he duly won the Eclipse, the King George and then the Arc to get his revenge and prove what a real champion he was. I watched the Arc at home with my father. We were both screaming at the TV in the final furlong and as Dancing Brave crossed the line in front, I not only had goose pimples but a lump in my throat and a tear in my eye.

It's hard to describe the emotion. The best that I can do is – pride. I will never forget Dancing Brave.

DEAN PHILLIPS, Newport, Gwent

The day I rode Arkle – and he was beaten
The 1966 Hennessy and childhood memories of a painful defeat for the greatest of them all

IT IS the last Saturday in November, the day of the 1966 Hennessy at Newbury.

I am perched in my usual position on the arm of Dad's chair (I rode a lot shorter in those days, not to mention lighter) with a rolled-up newspaper in my hand, just in case my selection needed any assistance.

The horses are at the start. Dad points out to me that there is a grey horse in the race, a fact that would usually sway my selection because greys are easier to follow on our black-and-white TV set.

However, today I'm not interested. Why? Because Arkle is running, and to this particular six-year-old Arkle is invincible. The race is soon under way, with the grey horse making the running, and though my heart is pounding, Pat Taaffe and I have 'Himself' under a tight rein.

Turning for home, and the grey appears to drop away and we take it up, victory in sight. What A Myth is giving chase when suddenly I'm aware that the grey horse hasn't dropped away at all. In fact, he's sat in Arkle's slipstream and I don't think Pat's noticed.

At the last, the grey pulls alongside, pounces, and sprints for the line. I pull my whip; Pat, at first reluctant to follow suit, pushes hands and heels. We start to close but it's too late: we're beaten.

In total disbelief, and with eyes quickly welling up, I turn to Dad, who, quickly assessing the situation, consoles me with words such as "massive weight concession" and "wonderful tactical ride by the winning jockey". He offers no suggestion that I might have ridden an ill-judged race.

These words reassure me that Arkle is still the greatest, but I gain two new heroes that day, Stalbridge Colonist and Stan Mellor. Even in defeat Arkle proved himself

the readers' choice **winning letters**

to be the greatest, trying to give such a great weight concession to two horses who, in any other era, would have been considered champions themselves.

GRAEME TAIT, Lincoln

Not news of a death but joy at Dawn Run
The 1986 Cheltenham Gold Cup – as heard by a racing fan far away on another continent

I LISTENED to Dawn Run's victory in the 1986 Cheltenham Gold Cup on the World Service while working as a volunteer teacher in rural Zambia.

I had managed to get a bet of 200 kwacha – then two weeks' allowance – with a Dutch bookmaker in the capital Lusaka. As they jumped the last I had given up hope, but the commentary on her comeback to snatch victory and the first Champion Hurdle/Gold Cup double in history led me to run out screaming into the corridor of the mission where I was staying.

One of the priests said afterwards that he thought I had received news of a sudden death, as I was so hysterical.

The build-up to the double attempt in the media, the excitement of the finish with the jubilation of the Dawn Run camp and the despair of the connections of Wayward Lad, and the celebrations afterwards will live forever in my memory. It was the top race I have ever experienced.

VINCE MURRAY, County Sligo, Ireland

Mandarin and Winter can't be surpassed
A miraculous performance from horse and rider in the 1962 Grand Steeple-Chase de Paris

FOR THE last 50 years I have been a passionate racing fan and have enjoyed all aspects of the sport, from point-to-points to Royal Ascot. I have also raced in Hong Kong and been to Australia for the Melbourne Cup.

But for me, there is no question as to what was the greatest race of all during this time – and I have seen it only on film – and that was the 1962 Grand Steeple-Chase de Paris. The winner was the 11-year-old Mandarin, ridden by Fred Winter, who got home by a head from the French horse Lumino. However, it is what happened in the race that makes it so remarkable and so memorable.

For one thing, it later emerged that Fred was severely debilitated by a stomach upset. And if this wasn't enough, Mandarin's bit broke after four fences. For the remaining three and a half miles, Fred was left without brakes or steering, as he had no contact with his mount's mouth.

Some of the French riders, aware of what was going on, helped Mandarin stay in the race by moving up on his outside going round the bends (the course consisted of two separate figures of eight). By sheer horsemanship and strength, Fred kept the horse in front, even though Mandarin broke down three fences from home. I have watched the race several times on film, and every time I see Mandarin hang on to win by the narrowest of margins – well, I just choke up. Of all the great races I have seen, it is the greatest.

ROY SIMPSON, Bournemouth

The 100-1 shot who fuelled my obsession
An enduring passion fostered by the 1990 Cheltenham Gold Cup and Norton's Coin

MY RACING obsession was born on Gold Cup day in 1990.

The most preposterous of sporting fairytales unfolded just as I was beginning my horseracing education. Naively crediting myself with more knowledge than could possibly be acquired in a few adolescent months, I 'knew' that 100-1 shots didn't win Gold Cups.

I explained this to my friend, who had never been in a bookie's before, giving him the full benefit of my new-found wisdom. He listened patiently, and then declared: "Yeah, but I just like the name Norton's Coin."

It is a race I will never tire of watching, again and again, either on videotape or more often in the cine-camera of my mind. It stands as a great monument to what can happen if you dare to dream. Norton's Coin stalked the leaders, took closer order as others (including the favourite Desert Orchid) faded, and in a final, exhilarating thrust, with the commentator's voice soaring and the jockey urging and straining and almost throwing his mount at the line, just prevailed over the unfortunate Toby Tobias.

My friend and I danced around the room like lunatics, like only the young and innocent can dance, not yet knowing that it wouldn't always be that easy, not yet knowing that we wouldn't always taste that glory, and not yet realising that, at the tender age of 18, we had already witnessed the greatest race of all time.

NEIL LIGHTNING, Wokingham, Berkshire

selected bibliography

The Racing Post

The Sporting Life

Timeform Racehorses/Chasers & Hurdlers annuals

A Century of Champions, by John Randall and Tony Morris
(Portway Press, 1999)

Notable English and Irish Thoroughbreds, edited by Mary Mountier
and Tony Morris (Alister Taylor & Genesis Publications, 1983)

Bloodstock Breeders' Review annuals 1912-1981

The History of the Derby Stakes, by Roger Mortimer (Cassell, 1962)

Big Red of Meadow Stable, by William Nack (Arthur Fields Books, 1975, available as
Da Capo Press paperback under the title *Secretariat: The Making of a Champion*)

Arkle – the story of a champion, by Ivor Herbert (Pelham Books, 1966, available as
Aurum Press paperback)

Red Rum, by Ivor Herbert (William Luscombe, 1974, available as Aurum Press
paperback)

Vincent O'Brien's Great Horses, by Ivor Herbert and Jacqueline O'Brien (Pelham Books,
1984)

The Winter Kings, by Ivor Herbert and Patricia Smyly (Pelham Books, 1989)

Oaksey on Racing – Thirty years of writing and riding, by John Oaksey (Kingswood
Press, 1991)

The Grey Horse: The True Story of Desert Orchid, by Richard Burridge (Pelham Books,
1992, available as Aurum Press paperback)

Frankie: The Autobiography of Frankie Dettori, with Jonathan Powell
(HarperCollinsWillow, 2004)

Horseracing's Greatest Ever Moments (video and DVD, Marks and Spencer, 2004)

Lester Piggott – My 12 Greatest Races (video, Castle Vision, 1991)